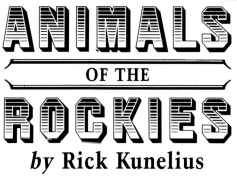

ANIMALS
OF THE
ROCKIES

by Rick Kunelius

ALTITUDE PUBLISHING
A

ACKNOWLEDGEMENTS

Many thanks to all the people who helped me to fill in the gaps in my knowledge bank, and to those who provided photographs to fill out the pages of this book.

Special thanks to Ken Preston who originally inspired this little book, and who did his best to teach me to spell and corrected my grammar throughout.

Animals of the Canadian Rockies
by Rick Kunelius
©Altitude Publishing Ltd. 1983
All Rights Reserved

ISBN 0-919381-07-3

CONTENTS

Mounted Specimens from the Sign of the Goat Curio, Elliott Barnes, 1907, photo courtesy of the Whyte Foundation, Archives of the Canadian Rockies

INTRODUCTION

THE PERCEPTION OF WILDLIFE has changed significantly over the years that people have been coming to the Rocky Mountains of Canada. The early explorers saw wildlife as a necessary food source for survival, as an economic commodity for their support and in some instances, as a threat to themselves and their domestic animals. Very few of the explorers and settlers ever considered the native animals as objects to be appreciated and preserved, except as dried meat for later consumption. Wildlife, in short, was to be used.

The establishment of Canada's first National Park at Banff in 1885 had little to do with the preservation of wildlife. The park was formed to provide controlled development of the mineral hot springs which would encourage tourist traffic on the recently completed railroad, and generate dollars for the federal treasury.

The first legal survey of Rocky Mountains Park (later Banff National Park) in 1886, enclosed an oblong block of land only 26 by 10 miles. Roughly, it comprised Sulphur Mountain, the Bow Valley across to include Cascade Mountain, Lake Minnewanka, and the mountains immediately east of the lake. The Commissioner of Fisheries at Ottawa was sent to inspect the new Reserve and report upon the condition of the game and fish. Mr. Whitcher found that large game and fish were scattered and comparatively scarce in contrast to earlier reports of wildlife abundance. Though he did not range far from Banff, he felt his findings were indicative of the general mountain area.

Mr. Whitcher foresaw the value of preserving the native wildlife and recommended that restricted hunting seasons and habitat improvements be initiated to protect and increase the dwindling resource. His vision was to establish a somewhat landscaped area that would harbour fish and wildlife, but from which would be excluded all beasts that preyed upon the game animals or were offensive to people. These included wolves, coyotes, foxes, lynxes, skunks, weasels, wild cats, porcupines and badgers. Bears were to be tolerated since they were primarily vegetarian and were not a problem. The other small animals and birds were to be left alone as they were "living ornaments interesting to visitors".

The early visitors to the mountain parks were expected to enjoy themselves in a leisurely fashion and did not travel through the back-country areas in large numbers. In order to facilitate the leisurely viewing of wildlife, a museum was established in Banff townsite. A zoo was developed adjacent to the museum, and on the broad flats east of

Don Harmon Feeding a Deer, Byron Harmon, ca. 1920, photo courtesy of the Whyte Foundation, Archives of the Canadian Rockies

Banff. It became well known and prominent benefactors donated numerous animals, some of which had nothing to do with the area, such as a polar bears, yaks and exotic pheasants.

The zoo was an outstanding attraction for the first third of the century. During this period of time park boundaries expanded, motor roads were developed and the native wildlife population increased in response to improved protection and good habitat. Many of the animals previously seen only in cages could now be seen along the roads and trails, notably sheep, goats, bears, elk, moose and deer. It was decided that a zoo inside of a living museum was inconsistant and in 1937 the zoo was closed.

Upon completion of the motor roads in the late twenties which linked Banff, Yoho, and Kootenay Parks, the department published a series of booklets encouraging the general public to enjoy the new roads and magnificent parks.

"For 175 miles the motorist is never outside of a National Park, a fact which reveals itself soon in the abundance and fearlessness of

335 CINNAMON BEAR.

The Zookeeper at the Banff Zoo Feeding a Cinnamon Bear, Byron Harmon, photo courtesy of the Whyte Foundation, Archives of the Canadian Rockies

the wild life. Mountain sheep, those shyest of wild creatures, lift their heads to gaze unconcernedly at the intruder and then go back to their quiet feeding. A deer will flash through the thick tangle of the forest or a black bear amble off from a leisurely inspection of the recent site of some wayside camp, but the wild things here are no longer afraid of man. They realize within these boundaries he has laid aside his ancient enmity and they are quick to offer in return the gift of equal friendship...."

"Kootenay National Park"., ca.1928

The newly established roads were the pride of the park service and by the mid-thirties they were even claimed as beneficial to wildlife.

"It is noticeable that the animals follow the roads and trails into the park, and, since the construction of the Banff-Windermere highway, large numbers of game have come in from British Columbia. From Exshaw to the Gap is a sheep country; elk and deer are found from the Gap to Banff, and deer, sheep, goat, moose and elk in the country west of Banff...."

M.B. Williams, *The Heart of the Rockies*, n.d.

As game in general became more abundant it was common to see elk, moose, bears and especially deer within the park townsites. As Mabel Williams wrote at the time;

"...During the winter the deer wander through the streets of Banff, poking their noses about the back doors of the residents, looking for scraps of food or that irresistable deer delicacy, potato

Mountain Goat Byron Harmon, photo courtesy of the Whyte Foundation, Archives of the Canadian Rockies

At the Banff Dump, photo courtesy of the Whyte Foundation, Archives of the Canadian Rockies

peeling. It is a common but pretty sight to see them feeding from the hands of children, a practise which is discouraged by park officials...."

M.B. Williams, *The Heart of the Rockies*, n.d.

Children may have been discouraged from feeding the animals but the same did not always apply to adults. For many years signs directed motorists to the local dumps where they could observe bears feeding on human scraps. The dumps naturally attracted concentrations of bears close to the townsites where they would seek fresher scraps from garbage cans, rather than compete for older garbage at the dumps. Bears at a distance minding their own business are quite acceptable, but bears in your backyard are dangerous. Too many people around too many bears inevitably led to problems. Over the years a growing number of people were injured by both black and grizzly bears. The perception changed gradually from bears as friendly, to bears as dangerous. Dumps were closed to the public in the early seventies, and people are now told to avoid bears for their own protection.

The literature of the thirties clearly stated that the national parks were famous game sanctuaries and hunting was completely outlawed. The parks were a paradise for wildlife with the exception of the predators such as wolves, cougars, wolverines, lynx, coyotes and hawks which the wardens were encouraged to dispatch. (They were a threat to the other species.) The parks were such effective sanctuaries, and the big game species had made such a comeback, that animals were leaving the parks to find more living space. Hunters were encouraged to use the park townsites as outfitting centers from which, in a two or three day trail trip, the best big game districts could be reached, adjacent to the park boundaries.

Black Bear, Byron Harmon, photo courtesy of the
Whyte Foundation, Archives of the Canadian Rockies

Forest fires and logging had opened much of the timbered areas of
the Bow Valley around the time of the construction of the railway.
These areas had recovered by the 'thirties to be prime, lush game
habitat. The trees were young, timber was small and wild animals
could be seen easily in abundance. Range conditions were so good that
the 250 elk which were transplanted to the Bow Valley about 1920 had
increased to an estimated 3000 in the early 'forties. Unfortunately the
masses of elk were cropping range which they shared with the sheep
and deer. The world within the parks was becoming overcrowded.
With the removal of predators, the ban on hunting, and the forests re-
establishing themselves, we had done too good a job of protecting the
wildlife.

The early park wardens were primarily concerned with forest
protection through fire suppression. Keeping trails open and patrolling
for fires, to extinguish them before they grew out of control, comprised their main duty. As tourist numbers increased their talents were
directed to servicing lookout stations, selling camping permits and
fishing licences, and hauling firewood to campgrounds, as well as their
normal patrol and general maintenance duties. It was not until a major
sheep die-off occurred in the early forties, while at the same time the

ranges were becoming over-populated with elk, that the wardens were reorganized to direct more attention to wildlife. As the chief warden of Banff, K.B. Mitchell wrote in the mid-forties; "We cannot blame the Wardens for not taking a greater interest in game as they also for the most part adopted an attitude of complacency in line with the general public."

Everyone enjoyed the early years of inflation of wildlife populations, but when the sheep died-off and elk were less than a dime a dozen, it was time for new management strategies. The zoo had been closed mainly because there was no longer a need for it, but the next phase of wildlife management was indeed ironic. Between 1944 and 1964 about 3000 elk were slaughtered in the Bow valley and its environs. It was an attempt to keep them from overgrazing the available range and suffering a similar catastrophic die-off to the sheep. The so-called balance-of-nature was judged to be out-of-balance.

Wolves were unknown in Banff Park prior to the 'forties, but once started it did not take them long to become widely established due to the excessive number of game animals available for them to prey on. It is probably safe to say that the number of wolves went from zero to sixty within the decade. Even though they assisted the wardens in reducing game populations, a provincial outbreak of rabies in the early 'fifties, and the terrifying thought of rabid wolves close to people, resulted in a programme of genocide against the wolves and coyotes.

The cold war on elk, wolves and coyotes continued through the 'fifties, but gradually died out in the early 'sixties as the balance of numbers in the big game populations began to be re-established. Even today no one really knows what these numbers are or in fact how the balance works. The 'sixties were a period of reflection and research. A new consciousness became established which recognized the role of predators in the nature of things. Catastrophic die-offs and over-grazing of rangelands was to be viewed as natural, and bears were to be weened off garbage. Animals, after all, were not so different from people. If they over-exploited their natural resources, catastrophies were bound to happen.

It almost seems that the conclusions of the 'sixties cut off wildlife research in the 'seventies. The emphasis of the later decade was bear behaviour and attempts at understanding the population numbers and dispersal patterns of the major animals.

In 1963 a new predator arrived in the form of the Trans-Canada Highway through Banff Park to again mess with the balances. Combined highway and railway mortalities between 1964 and 1980 resulted

Mule Deer, Carl Rungius, (1869-1959), pencil sketch on paper, courtesy of the Whyte Foundation, Peter Whyte Gallery

Mountain Goat, Carl Rungius, (1869-1959), etching on paper, courtesy of the Whyte Foundation, Peter Whyte Gallery

Mounted Heads in The Sign of the Goat Curio, Elliott Barnes, 1906, photo courtesy of the Whyte Foundation, Archives of the Canadian Rockies

in the death of 120 moose, 649 elk, 400 mule deer, and 129 sheep, to name only the major species affected. The problem with highway and railway mortalities is that they cannot be considered natural, and they result in excessive property and human damage. They are unnatural catastrophes which hopefully can be prevented.

It is difficult to predict what the consciousness of the 'eighties will produce. The forests are getting older and becoming thicker, and it has been a long time since a major forest fire has opened significant areas of range land. The larger game animals are becoming harder to see and their numbers are likely to decrease with the corresponding growth of mature forests. The game fence being established in conjunction with the twinning of the Trans-Canada will reduce unnatural wildlife mortalities, and human property damage but the recent resurgence of wolves may find the fence an asset to normal hunting strategies. The new conservation consciousness might suggest that we hunt wild animals in National Parks to protect them from over-exploiting their own resources. Major fires may re-establish viewable wildlife ranges capable of supporting increased animal numbers once again.

National Parks are refuge to native animals in their natural state. Predators are free to roam and kill the other animals which they require for their own survival. In the long run they are beneficial and assist in keeping other populations under a certain degree of control. If periodic natural die-offs occur in some species they are no longer interferred with by man, in order that we can better understand the workings of nature. National Parks are intended to be living museums. The less we interfere with the natural processes of fire, vegetation and animals, the more we will come to understand how it all works without us.

Black Bear and Cubs Byron Harmon, photo courtesy of the Whyte Foundation, Archives of the Canadian Rockies

In one short century we have changed from indiscriminate consumers of wildlife, through the overprotective parental phase, to finally begin to perceive wildlife as equals with us. To me, the ideal of the National Parks as wildlife sanctuaries can best be achieved if we respect the animals as individuals carrying out their own private lives. They are not here as servants to entertain us. If their activities coincide with ours, and fear is not present, magic moments can occur.

Rick Kunelius

Rick Kunelius
Park Warden
Banff National Park

Coyote Al Williams for Banff National Park

Muletail Deer Anders Lent

Nanny Goats With Kids Rick Kunelius

Cougar Bruno Engler

Hoary Marmot Carole Harmon

Red Squirrel Anders Lent

Wolverine H.U. Green

Black Bear and Cub Bruno Engler

overleaf: *Muletail Fawn* H.U. Green
overleaf inset: *Muletail Stag in Velvet* Bob Sandford

BEAR

Inspector Ryan and Black Bear on the Banff-Windermere Highway Byron Harmon, 1924, photo courtesy of the Whyte Foundation, Archives of the Canadian Rockies

THERE IS NO DOUBT about it, bears are dangerous. Most other wild animals wandering through a townsite or camp can be tolerated, and some even encouraged, but the potential of a harmful encounter with a bear is too great to chance. Comparing bears with dogs helps to establish a realistic perspective. Using the measurements of a coyote for an average size dog we get: weight 9-11 kg., shoulder height 50 cm. and length without tail 90 cm..

Adult black bears generally weigh between 55-135 kg. and are 1.2-1.5 m long. Shoulder height varies from 60-100 cm.. Standing on their hind legs they can easily reach 1.8 m. up a tree.

Grizzly bears grow much larger, and are overall more massive. Adult grizzlies range between 115-340 kg. and reach 1.5-2 m. from nose to tail. Shoulder height when down on all fours is 0.75-1.0 m. When an adult grizzly stands on its hind legs it can reach 2.75 m. up a tree without even stretching.

Dogs and bears are stable only when on all four legs. Consequently their only effective tool is their mouths. The old expression "go for the throat" comes from watching dogs fighting. When dogs play or fight they wrestle about with their jaws. And so it is with bears. Many an old bear walks about with facial scars inflicted more from bites than from claws.

When a bear investigates an object his primary tool is his mouth. Paws are used to roll and move objects which the mouth cannot grasp or needs assistance with. It is very rarely that a bear will attempt to pick-up an object with its paws to examine it visually. Thinking back to dogs again, does a dog pick-up a toy with its paws or with its mouth?

So it is that when a bear decides it is time to investigate a person in greater detail he tends to use his most effective tool, namely his mouth. The power inherent in the jaws of a bear far exceeds that required to damage human flesh. A German Shepherd dog can effectively break a man's forearm in a determined attack, or easily mutilate fleshy parts beyond recognition.

Grizzly Bear, Carl Rungius, (1869-1959), etching on paper, courtesy of the Whyte Foundation, Peter Whyte Gallery

The average black bear easily outweighs and probably out-powers such a dog by at least three times.

Even bear cubs, as cute and cuddly as they may appear, should not be played with. Aside from the fact that the mother bear is usually close by, they are miniature power houses by themselves. I've tried to hold down a cub which was under a net and at the further disadvantage of coming out of a state of drug tranquilization. It was all I could do to hold the little cub down while my partner injected another dose of tranquilizing drug. Cubs are the equivalent of adult German Shepherd dogs, another animal I'd never attempt to take on bare handed.

The best place to safely observe bears is in a zoo or at a distance safely contained within a car which can rapidly leave the scene if the bear becomes aggressive. If the bear is not in a cage, it is a good idea to have a cage around yourself.

Black bears differ from grizzly bears firstly by being noticeably smaller. Black bears are not always black, quite often they may be cinnamon or brown. A black mother might even have one brown and one black cub. Brothers and sisters can be quite different. Grizzly bears are usually a shade of brown, yellowish brown or tawny and have grizzled (whitish) hair tips on some parts of their bodies, usually over the front shoulders. Some grizzlies can be such

a dark brown that they appear almost black. Color is not always a good criteria for separating the species, except to say that no one has ever recorded a shiny jet black grizzly, a color common to black bears.

Features to watch for to distinguish the species are as follows: black bears have a straight facial profile and tapered nose while grizzlies have a concave (dished) face and straight nose. The black bear carries its head high and presents a straight shoulder-rump line across the back while the grizzly has a hump over its shoulder and the head is carried lower presenting a broken profile when walking. Black bears have short sharply curved claws adapted for climbing while grizzlies have longer less sharply-curved claws more adapted for digging.

Bears, like people, are omnivorous eaters consuming both plant and animal material and capable of surviving on a meat or vegetable diet. They can eat anything that people eat and dearly love to feed on human garbage. I was once examing bear scats near Banff townsite with a visiting biologist who was interested in what bears preferred to eat. Our list looked something like this: grass, horsetail plants, berries, bone fragments, plastic bags, more grass, corn kernels, roots, king crab shell, other berries, hair, more berries and butcher shop rib bits. The biologist expected to find human garbage included in scats found so close to town but what were king crab shells doing 600 miles from the coast? Very simply, one of the restaurants had recently added seafood to its menu.

Bear diets vary significantly with the seasons and type of vegetation locally available. When they first emerge from their dens in the spring, fresh green forage is rather sparse and they naturally prefer to feast on any available carcasses of winter killed elk, sheep or goats. Black bears work the lower elevations where new plants are emerging while grizzlies dig for the favorite roots of the hedysarum, spring beauty and glacier lilies at higher elevations.

Bears are not great hunters but they can sometimes manage to locate and catch newly born moose, elk and deer calves, as well as older animals weakened by winter which have not yet regained their strength. Various rodents serve as appetizers and grizzlies are sometimes seen tearing up hillsides after ground squirrels. Most digging is done in search of roots which are, after all, much easier to catch than ground squirrels.

A.O. Wheeler, T.G. Longstaff, and Three Dead Grizzlies, Byron Harmon, 1910, photo courtesy of the Whyte Foundation, Archives of the Canadian Rockies

As the summer progresses the bears eat their way through various types of plants, nipping off the most succulent parts when they are most nutritious. Black bears are often seen alongside roads merrily nipping off the yellow flowers of the dandelions. Favorite plants for the bears include: cow parsnip, glacier lily, horse tail, clover, and numerous grasses and forbs. Ants and larvae in old logs and under rocks are also highly prized. When the berries ripen in late summer bears consume large quantities of strawberry, buffalo berry, saskatoon, huckleberry, gooseberry and currant. If nuts are available in the fall they will happily consume all they can find, mostly pine nuts in the mountains. When the plants dry up and the berries are gone bears depend on roots again to put on their final layers of fat before hibernating.

Bear ranges vary significantly in size mostly depending upon the amount of available food. Some black bears are known to be happy staying within 2.6 km. sq. area though most must range over a much larger area to locate the required foods as they change through the seasons. The smallest recorded grizzly range was 26 km. sq. but many grizzly ranges are more in the neighborhood of 400 sq. km.. Bear ranges necessarily overlap but it is rare for bears to have exactly the same range. Males range out farther than females and some radio-collared males are known to range over a distance of 200 km. in a matter of a few days.

Bears can be found anywhere in the mountains from the lowest river valley to high above timberline at the limits of available vegetation.

Covered in thick dark fur, bears do not like to be out in the bright hot sun and often spend mid-day resting or sleeping in shallow earth beds in the cool shade of a tall conifer tree. During the active months, home to a bear is wherever it happens to lay down for a sleep. As the days become shorter and colder in the late fall bears search out appropriate locations and prepare dens to hibernate in order to avoid winter. Their systems do not digest dry grass or twigs, and not being efficient hunters, they sleep away the long cold northern winters when appropriate foods are not available.

Most bears do not come out of their dens during the winter, but some bears which have denned-up close to garbage dumps have been known to wake up occasionally and wander out for a monthly snack.

In the mountains, black bears usually den at low elevations taking advantage of whatever natural protection may be available, though bears are supposed to dig tunnels and chambers in the earth. Black bear dens can be natural caves or frost pockets, hollow trees or simple excavations between the roots of a big old tree.

27

They have been known to crawl under buildings and a couple were once found trying to avoid winter in the comfort of the old steam heating plant at Jasper Park Lodge. One particularly lazy bear once denned up in a culvert under the Mt. Norquay road.

On the other hand grizzly bears, with the exception of those who den near garbage dumps, seek seclusion. Their dens are located in the 2100 m. elevation range on the shady sides of the mountains where the snow drifts over and covers them with a thick insulating blanket until spring. Being natural born diggers they rarely compromise their dens for make shift shelters so characteristic of the blacks.

Most burrows and sleeping chambers are very spartan and the bears make do with a dirt floor. But there is always the odd, ambitious bear who will line its sleeping chamber with soft moss. Chamber size varies with the size of the bear as well as on whether cubs accompany the female bear. Males and females always den separately (except as cubs with their mother).

Bears mate in the spring time between late May and early July. As far as we know, males select but one female to mate with and brief though the courtship and copulation period may be, they do not try to impregnate as many females as they can while the season lasts. Bears have a peculiar adaptation in that the embryo does not implant and begin to grow immediately. The delayed implantation does not occur until late in the fall. It is thought that the embryo does not implant at all in bears which do not put on sufficient fat through the summer and fall with which to nurse their young through the last half of hibernation.

Normally, implantation occurs when the bear begins her hibernation in late November or early December. Young bears, usually twins, are born in late January or February. Nowhere, except in a bear family, is there so little commotion raised over a new arrival. The mother hardly even bothers to wake up. The young cubs are blind miniature replicas with a light coat of fur and weigh only 225-280 gm. if they are black, and about 400 gm. if they are grizzly. They definitely do not attempt to go outside into the

Grizzy Bear T.W. Hall for Banff National Park

cold winter but rather snuggle up to mom and merrily nurse away as the urge inspires them until spring time.

By the time spring arrives and the mother bear is ready to wake up out of hibernation, the cubs are grown enough to take on the outside world, with mother's help of course. They are well beyond the diaper stage. If human babies could be raised like that I'm sure we'd all have a different perspective on raising children.

Bears do not simply wake-up to a biological alarm clock and head out of their dens ready to take on another summer season. Rather they come out for a stretch, take a look around and think about whether it's really time to wake up or not. If it is warm and sunny they might establish a surface day bed near the den entrance for a few more winks, or if spring is slow in arriving they might just as likely go back into the den to sleep a while longer.

Even though the cubs are quite agile when they hit the slopes in the spring they have a lot to learn about the ways of the world. They are slow to grow and they stay close to the mother bear nursing regularly and learning what to eat and where to find it throughout the first summer. In the fall the sow digs an extra large den and they curl up together for their first winter. The next summer is also spent travelling with mom. By the time the second fall rolls around some independent well-grown young bears may den-up by themselves but they are more likely to take advantage of the extra comfort and remain as part of the family. When they emerge the second spring, the by now sub-adult youngsters are driven away to make their own living in the world, while the sow takes up with another mate and begins the cycle all over again.

When the cubs are with their mother they do not have much to fear from the world but when they take off on their own they become vulnerable. It is this sub-adult class of bears establishing themselves in the world which often gets into trouble not only with the older bears but with people as well. Similar to human teenagers they often push situations to see how far they can get. If they stumble upon a campground with easy pickings they are liable to hang around making the best for themselves and the worst for the inhabitants, rather than going to the additional effort of searching out the food they learned to appreciate when mom knew where to find it. Unless they are trapped and relocated or driven away physically they

may even come to associate humans with easy pickings and habitually come back for more. For the good of the bears it is best to not make human food and garbage available to them at any time.

Do not feed the bears. The hand that feeds could get eaten.

Aside from their sub-adult years when bears are not protected by their mothers and they have not reached adult proportions or established their own personal ranges to guarantee adequate food resources, bears have no natural enemies except other bears. The grizzly bear is the largest predator in the mountains and even adult black bears give them a wide berth whenever possible. Diseases take their toll but most bears have a good chance of living to their normal old age of about 18-22 years if they are not hunted or do not run afoul of people.

Encountering Bears

The most often asked question in any general discussion of bears always seems to be: "What do you do when you meet a bear face to face?" There is no perfect answer and what may work in one situation may backfire in another.

Some bear experts claim that the strategy differs if one encounters a black bear or a grizzly bear. Grizzly bears rarely climb trees, so if it's a grizzly then climb a tree, the worst he can do is stand at the bottom and shake you out. Black bears are rarely aggressive so stand your ground and outbluff them. Age and sex of the bear is also a factor in how it will react (this may also be true of the person as well). There is an undeniable fact that many alleged bear experts have made mistakes in identifying the species at various times, let along being able to rapidly age and sex them at the moment of truth. In general it is best to admit that a bear is a bear and regardless of the species or sex, it is more powerful than any un-armed person.

Numerous strategies have developed over the years and each has its own band of supporters. But there always appears someone who can testify that the solution did not work in his particular encounter, or one that he knows of intimately. My own solution is a mix of recipes tempered by my own peculiar perspective and system of logic. The following strategy makes the best sense to me and has proven effective in a limited number of encounters. However, there is no guarantee.

The best solution is to avoid the encounter. Make your presence known. When possible move in the open where you have a chance to see the bear ahead of time, or where it can more easily see, hear or smell you, and correspondingly avoid you.

Better yet, ride a horse. Horses have better perception in the wilderness than people. They can often smell a bear before either they or you actually see it, and they are simply more aware of what is going on in the woods. Bears are not known to attack horses and there is no documented case to my knowledge of anyone on horseback ever suffering un unprovoked bear attack.

Making your presence known to bears before you encounter them can be accomplished by whistling, talking, singing or carrying bells as you hike along the trail. This strategy has obvious short-comings if you are walking a trail which follows alongside a noisy stream or if a strong wind is blowing. Moreover a good deal of the pleasure of being out in the woods is enjoying the quiet and listening for the sounds of birds and other forest creatures. Some woodsmen ridicule bear bells claiming that they merely function as a pleasant announcement to the bears that lunch is coming.

If you have a dog that has grown-up with bears, and if it happens to have that rare quality that it would risk its own life for yours, such a dog could be of benefit to travel with in bear country. Dogs, like horses, will usually discover any bears well ahead of you. However, where bears are known to not attack horses they are also well known to take on any dog that comes along. After all, the bear is looking at a potentially simple meal in a dog. When traveling with a dog in bear country the owner should always consider: what if the dog encounters a bear well ahead on the trail and instead of driving it away merely manages to infuriate it? Chances are the bear will put the chase on the dog, rather than vice versa, and the dog will come running back to its master for protection and security with the bear hot on its heels.

If you see a bear well ahead of you on the trail or coming your direction across an open area, climb a tree as high as you can. Remember some grizzlies can easily reach up to 3 m. high. Grizzlies (except as cubs) cannot climb trees unless the branches happen to be conveniently spaced so they can drape their paws over them like a ladder. A black bear will not likely have

reason to climb up after you unless you are dripping with sardines and honey. Watch where the bear goes from your safe perch and give it ample time to pass far away. When you decide it is safe to descend try to go in the opposite direction to which the bear went. Put a few good miles between yourself and the spot where you were treed before setting up camp.

When camping, keep your camp clean. Cook and wash-up away from your tent so that food droppings and cooking grease do not become associated with your tent or bed roll. Cache your food up a tree in a watertight container well away from your camp. If you are motoring keep your food sealed-up and stashed securely in the trunk of your car.

If you are unlucky enough to run into a bear in the woods without time to climb a tree, or without a climbable tree at hand DO NOT RUN. Keep your cool and start talking to yourself. It doesn't matter what you talk about, the bear can't understand you anyway, but it does help to calm your nerves.

The problem with running is that it might just provoke pursuit. A bear which was merely approaching out of curiosity, or simply unaware, suddenly has something to react to. If you merely stand there the reaction can be calm and unhurried, giving the bear time to make up its own mind what to do. Generally the bear will simply establish what you are and carry on its own way. If you run, the bear may feel it has to run after you and knock you down to assure itself that the disappearing form does not mean trouble. If it is a sow and cubs, fast action may startle the bears with the attendant result that the cubs take off in different directions and the sow does not immediately know where they are and that the cubs are safe. Anything which threatens her cubs will be dealt with in the most direct manner at her disposal. And if that means you, look out!

You can't out-run a bear. A bear can even out-run a horse for a short distance, though it can't keep it up. The old saying that bears cannot run well going downhill is not always true. An old warden in Banff once witnessed a bear take down a deer on a downhill chase.

The stories say that Daniel Boone ''grinned down a bear'' and they may not be so far off. Alberta's Andy Russell who has spent more time with grizzly bears than anyone I am aware of unequivocally states; ''...Even a thoroughly angry grizzly will not attack a person who

Grizzly Banff National Park

Grizzly Sow and Cubs, Carl Rungius, (1869-1959), etching on paper, courtesy of the Whyte Foundation, Peter Whyte Gallery

stands his ground and faces the animal...''. An occasion may happen which proves an exception, but Andy is still alive and until now he hasn't been proven wrong.

If your find you can't simply stand your ground and talk or grin down the bear, then slowly back away and allow the bear unimpeded access along his way. If your pack is reeking of available food you might quietly and slowly slip it off and leave it for the bear. Move smoothly; quick jerky motions will only incite the bear to move quickly. Think of the cops and robbers shows you've seen, the guys that stay cool and don't make any fast moves don't usually get shot.

Andy makes one other logical point concerning close-range encounters. Bears normally walk on all four legs. Even the grizzly bear which is sometimes called ''the beast that walks like a man'' only walks upright on its back legs for very short distances. The upright position is associated as one of curiosity and fearlessness. The upright standing position of a bear is not a fighting stance.

What follows from this observation is simply that you do not lie down and play dead unless you have been knocked down. Getting into the prone position may be construed by the bear as moving into combat position, until you are actually prone.

If you are knocked down, or if you are already down because you fainted or were in your sleeping bag, stay face down. Cover your neck with clasped hands and keep your elbows out away from your body. With your elbows out the bear will not be able to roll you over unless it makes a very determined effort. Only in extremely rare circumstances will a bear make more than a cursory investigation of a person before moving on about its normal business of making a living.

If you are still a bit leary about travelling in bear country, but do not want to pass up the chance of enjoying the great outdoors in the mountains, there are some positive steps which can be taken to minimize any chance of trouble with the bears. Travel on horseback or at least with a group of several persons. There is some safety in numbers. Find out from the park wardens or wilderness personnel where known bear areas are and avoid them. If you can afford it, travel with an organized guided group. If public shelters or commercial lodges exist plan to stay in them or camp close by so you can flee to an island of safety if a bear problem occurs in the area.

BEAVER

Beaver Joe Benge

 EAVERS HAVE SMALL HEADS, tiny legs and not an overly large body but when you pick them up by the tail it feels as if you've just latched on to a sack of cement. In reality the average adult beaver weighs 23-28 kg.. Their roundish oval body grows 0.9-1.2 m. long and the flat, black, hairless, scaly, leathery tail averages 30 cm. Height at the shoulder is about 30 cm. They are evenly colored over the back in rich tones from reddish chestnut to a deep rich brown, with the undersides being slightly paler. Since they do most of their travelling in water the short legs and heavy bodies are compensated by the buoyancy factor, but if they had to spend more time on land they'd probably look a lot different with thinner bodies and perhaps longer legs. Average life span of a beaver is 10-12 years.

Beavers have automatic valves in their nose and ears which close when they go under water and open again when they surface. They probably see better underwater than they do on land. Though they cannot live under water they can stay submerged for as long as 15 minutes before coming up for a fresh supply of air. Beavers are powerful swimmers with their large webbed toed hind feet. Their broad flat tail can be used to scull about slowly. The tail also acts as a balancing leg when they are cutting down trees or carrying mud above water level. The tail is most famous as the social warning clapper, resounding for long distances when a beaver slaps the water surface as an alarm before diving for safety.

Beavers are solely vegetarian but their choice of vegetable matter is hardly appetizing. Only secondarily do they indulge in succulent stream-side plants and aquatic vegetation. For most of the year they eat the bark of poplar trees, willow shrubs and a few miscellaneous bush species. Adventuresome beavers will also eat the lower boughs of pine, cedar, spruce or fir trees for a bit of variation.

Since beavers cannot climb trees like porcupines, they must bring the trees down to their own level. No tree is too big for these little lumberjacks to try their teeth at, but they generally specialize in trees of 20 cm. diameter or less. Bigger trees mean more work for less reward, because they have to be cut up to transportable sizes for consumption back home.

When felling a tree a beaver does not simply bite out chunks of wood until it falls down. Only the lower incissors are cutting tools. Each chip is a three stage process. Standing up on its hind legs, using its' tail for a brace, it cuts a notch, and then drops about 7 cm. to cut another notch below the first one. Then it grabs it with both sets of teeth and wrenches the wood chip out. Systematically it works around the entire tree cutting deeper and deeper until the tree is ready to break of its own weight. They cannot control the direction of fall, but luckily most trees growing along a stream bank lean naturally toward the water and the tree falls in the most convenient direction.

Beaver range is dependent upon available watercourses and accessible food supply. Once they locate a favorable area where they can become initially established, they quickly set to work building dams and cutting canals to enlarge the amount of favorable terrain available to themselves and succeeding family generations. Some beavers locate in large streams or rivers which are too big to dam and are of sufficient year round depth that they do not require improvement. In these situations they merely burrow a home into the bank rather than build a house. In the mountains where streams tend to be shallow and the water volume varies greatly with the seasons, most beavers resort to dam building and house construction in order to survive.

Similar to the moose and to a lesser degree the elk, beaver depend upon successional vegetation to survive. They rarely can find enough of their required foods in mature coniferous forests, so their distribution is affected by the previous fire history of an area. Early explorers left no record of encountering beaver in the mature forests of the mountains, but in 1920 after the extensive fires of the late 19th century, beaver were discovered in the Bow Valley near Altrude Creek. The populations expanded slowly colonizing areas of sub-climax aspen growth, and in the early fifties population pressures had spread the beaver up the tributary streams to altitudes of 2100-2200 m. Because forest fires were so effectively suppressed in the national parks during the 20th Century, beavers are not now overly abundant.

Beavers expand their habitat through damming and back flooding low lying ares which allow water dependant plants such as the willow to correspondingly extend their range. The beaver thereby provides not only more food for himself, but also for other browsing animals such as the moose and deer.

Beaver dams fulfill a multi-function purpose. They provide sufficient water to float food home, allow easy access to food source areas, escape from predators and finally a home building site and underwater food storage area. The ponds must be deep enough that when they freeze over in the winter there is still sufficient water below the ice for the beavers to swim to their submerged food caches. They do not venture out above ground during winter.

Winter food is stored by pulling branches and trunk sections to the bottom of the pond and securing the ends in the bottom mud. Food which is cut early in the summer, is sometimes left to sink by itself as it becomes waterlogged. If there is not sufficient mud at the bottom of the pond, rocks are used to hold down the food supply. Additional branches can be stuffed into the sunken jumble.

Beaver lodges are constructed so that the living chamber is slightly above high water level and the entrance hole is below the deepest ice level. In this way home is always dry and accessible throughout the year. The thick impenetrable dome of sticks and mud above the living chamber provides good insulation against the winter cold. Home renovations or expansion can be carried out at any time removing mud and biting out branches or adding wood and mud plaster to the outside. The interior bed-living room of a large family may be as big as 1.2-1.5 m. across and 1 m. high. Exterior dimensions of old established lodges have been found to measure 10 m. in diameter and 2 m. high.

Occasionally a lodge may be home to only one beaver but communal group size might extend to twelve. Usually a lodge is assumed to contain six beaver; the mother and father and two offspring from each of their two previous litters.

Beavers seemingly mate for life. They breed when the nights are long in January or February; the young are born almost four months later. Just before the new litter arrives, the two year old children are kicked-out of the lodge to set-up their own quarters and the father moves out temporarily. Home is made a bit fancier with the inclusion of a soft bed made ready for the new arrivals. Average litter size is three or four furry little open-eyed replicas about 30 cm. long, weighing about 0.5 kg. apiece. They have an inherent ability to swim and it is not long before they are following the family around learning to fend for themselves. Older family members supply food.

When beavers are in their home pond close to or within their almost bomb-proof lodges, they have nothing to fear from mountain predators. But when exposed on dry land searching for distant vegetation their slow speed makes them vulnerable to bears, wolverines, coyotes, wolves, cougars, and occasionally the little lynx. If they can't construct swimming channels out to the feed areas they may be forced to abandon the home site and rebuild elsewhere or risk extermination. Abandoned beaver ponds often exist for years after the beavers leave, continuing to provide habitat for fish and birds and helping in water conservation and flood control.

Buffalo Bulls Byron Harmon, photo courtesy of the Whyte Foundation, Archives of the Canadian Rockies

BUFFALO

B UFFALO OR "BISON" NEVER were overly common in the mountains, but buried skulls and bone fragments show that they did visit, if not regularly inhabit, most of the low major valleys. An attempt to re-introduce buffalo into the northern parts of Jasper Park in the mid-seventies failed when the buffalo, on their own accord, decided to leave the mountainous park lands for greener pastures to the east. A small herd is kept in an enclosure near Banff townsite for public viewing from motor vehicles. Though apparently peaceable and adapted to people they are still wild animals and should not be approached on foot.

Buffalo are darkish brown with massive frontquarters covered with longer hair than the rest of the body. Both male and female carry permanent short black horns. An adult bull may weigh up to 900 kg. while a female weights in at a mere 450 kg. The bulls can grow to almost 3 m. long and stand 1.7-2.0 m. at the shoulder. Cows are correspondingly smaller standing only 1.4-1.7 m. tall. Females can be distinguished from males by their smaller, more rounded hump, narrower head and relatively short beard. Protected buffalo live to about 15 years of age.

Buffalo are grazers, consuming enormous amounts of grasses and sedges. Similar to moose, elk and deer, they do not have upper front teeth (incisors). They are well adapted with a great digestive ability for living off poor quality grasses and they are not overly particular about what kind of grass they eat. In winter their large heads act like snow shovels clearing the snow away to get at the grass below. In the Banff enclosure, where range is limited, they are fed hay during the winter.

Mountain range requirements are not known since we do not have any free ranging herds. Home to a buffalo is anywhere grassy in the great outdoors. They seek protection in forested areas during severe winter conditions and on days of intense summer sun.

Buffalo are very gregarious and intermix freely throughout the year. Some old bulls may range off by themselves for a while and numerous bachelor groups develop for short periods. Bison are sexually mature at three or four years but very few bulls do any breeding before seven years. They breed throughout the summer with the larger bulls servicing most of the cows. There is some fighting between the bulls during the rut but they do not attempt to form harems which would require aggresive defensive reactions.

Single calves are born nine months later. They are originally a reddish-tan changing to dark brown at about three months of age. There are no hidden nursery thickets or fancy birth places. When the time comes the cow merely moves off a short distance from the herd to deliver her calf. Similar to domestic cattle the calf is up wobbling about within a few hours of birth and in two or three days mother and calf are back moving with the herd. They are generally weaned by fall though some cows may continue to lactate and provide extra nourishment for their calves throughout the winter.

One has only to face a buffalo head on to realize that it has no natural enemies and has no need to run from trouble. Even grizzly bears and wolves are capable of culling only badly weakened animals. Diseases which often prove fatal to buffalo include tuberculosis, anthrax, and brucellosis. Internal and external parasites appear to have very little significant effect upon these massive creatures.

CHIPMUNK

Chipmunk Rick Kunelius

HERE ARE NUMEROUS SPECIES of chipmunks but they all have similar characteristics and habits. They are noticeably small than Columbian Ground Squirrels, larger than the pikas, and just a bit smaller than the red squirrels. An average size chipmunk would be 28 cm. in length, including a 9 cm. tail. They stand about 5 cm. tall at the shoulder and weigh only 230 gm.

The most distinguishing feature of the chipmunks is the black and white stripes which run down their backs. Color patterns vary with the species but the coat always carries a blend of earth tones. Males and females look the same.

Chipmunks eat a wide variety of plant foods and numerous insects. Favorite insects include ants, bees, grasshoppers, caterpillers and spiders. They love mushrooms and the tender shoots and flowers of dandelions and low growing willows. When berries are in season they consume any kind of berry they can reach. Their tiny claws are extremely adept at handling seeds which they examine carefully before quickly husking them with their needle-sharp teeth.

Dried foods which will keep well are transported to the home burrow or deposited in numerous caches in the vicinity of home. High capacity carrying is managed with their expandable cheek pouches. Some exuberant naturalists have painstakingly recorded chipmunk carrying capacities and have come up with the following figures: 112 cherry pits, 162 cactus seeds, 264 buckbrush seeds, 1650 wild cranberry seeds, and 2100 veronica seeds. One can only assume that these were adult chipmunks they were following.

Chipmunks do not range any noticeable distance beyond home burrow range. They are not adapted to digging with their delicate little paws and depend on finding rotting logs, loose soil or jumbled rocks in which they can piece together passageways and excavate modest burrows.

They disappear into their underground homes in the fall and though slowing down their pace, they remain active all winter gradually consuming their stored provisions. When the first tender plants begin growing in the spring they appear above ground and soon locate a mate.

The gestation period is about one month and litter sizes average five naked, pink, blind little squeekers. After a week of nursing, their stripes begin to appear under their skin just ahead of the fine fuzzy fur. They are not mobile until they are at least two weeks old and their eyes do not open until they are a full month old, when they are ready to face the outside world. At two months they are off setting up their own homes and making their own living. They rarely go far to set up housekeeping and happily share territories and just about everything else, except their bedrooms and private food stocks.

Chipmunks are very fast and agile which is a good thing since they are a highly prized meal to numerous predators such as coyotes, wolves, badgers, cougars, weasels, hawks and eagles. Living in close proximity to each other, if one senses danger he quickly alerts the others with a rapid shrill call which results in everyone heading for cover.

COUGAR

FAMOUS AMERICAN COUGAR hunter, Jay Bruce, is said to have travelled 40,000 miles on foot chasing cougars over the years, and in that time saw only one that was not already treed by a dog. Cougars are uncommon throughout the Rockies although they do range along the eastern slopes and you might be one of the lucky few who gets a fleeting glimpse of this magnificent cat.

The color of an adult cougar varies in solid tones of yellow, brown, red or gray. Males weigh about 70 kg. and females are correspondingly lighter at 45 kg. Males often grow to 2.5 m. in length and females to about 30 cm. less. Of course about 1 m. of this length includes their long tubular looking furry tail. The cougar's average life span is about ten years.

Cougars or mountain lions are incredibly strong, especially through their front shoulders and hindquarters. They attack explosively, often knocking their victims to the ground. Teeth and claws are both adapted for tearing and slashing. The claws are constructed in such a way that the harder a victim tries to struggle away, the deeper and more firmly the claws grasp.

Cougar paws are well padded helping them to stalk quietly. The back paw is smaller than the front and often steps into the front paw imprint, allowing the cougar to be even more stealthy.

Cougars are carnivorous (meat eaters) but they do regularly consume grass. The grass is often regurgitated, perhaps to reduce the parasite load which builds up in their stomachs. There appears to be no animal which cougars will not eat given the chance. Their favorite food is deer, and cougar are not known to range where deer are not available. Though they rarely attack adult bears they will take a cub if the opportunity arises. When hungry and not successful with other animals they will eat even skunks and porcupines.

Whether they eat large or small mammals depends of course on availability and individual hunting skill. When hunting, cougars carefully stalk to within 15 m. of the intended victim before making a final explosive rush. If the victim's neck is not broken upon impact, the neck or throat is quickly torn open with a rapid bite. The victim is then carried or dragged away to a secluded spot before being feasted upon. Cougars tear open the belly of the victim, consuming first the liver, heart and lungs. If the animal is small or the cougar extremely hungry it may consume the animal in one sitting. More often it will cover the remainder of the carcass with forest litter or grass and return to feed upon it later, as long as the meat has not begun to spoil. Spoiled remains are left for such scavengers as bears, coyotes and birds. Cougars hunt both during the day and at night.

Cougars, appear to have established ranges within which they hunt. Average range for a male is about 65-90 sq. km. while females work smaller ranges of about 40-80 sq. km. Some radio-collared lions were found to travel 40 km. in a days wanderings within their range. They travel both during the day and at night and may occasionally take to swimming though they seem to share the common feline aversion to water.

They are solitary animals with the exception of brief periods when courting or rearing young. Though cougars can mate and bear young at any time during the year, they naturally time their actions so that the kittens are born during the more favorable months. Since they are spread very sparsely throughout their range, there is little competition or selection availability for mating. Males accompany females for a short period during mating but are soon driven away to continue their solitary existence.

The gestation period is about three months, at which time the female finds a small rough natural den to bear her kittens. Litter size is usually two or three small, furry, spotted kittens of about 30 cm. in length, each weighing about .5 kg.

Cougar Bruno Engler

The male is not welcomed back to see his off-spring as he would be more likely to eat them than help to find food for them. After about ten days of nursing the eyes of the little kittens open and they become quite mobile. At six or seven weeks the mother is leading the young kittens out to feed on nearby kills.

By the time the kittens are eight months old they weigh about 22 kg. are 1.2-1.5 m. long, and are well on their way to becoming effective killers, however, they still have a lot to learn and may stay with their mothers for an additional year's schooling.

Cougars have no natural enemies and are rarely subject to disease since they maintain clean habits, move about continuously and live separately. They are subject to accidental death from injuries received from their victims such as piercing hooves or horns of large animals, and occasionally, too many quills from a porcupine.

COYOTE

HE "LITTLE WOLF," or "bush wolf" as he is commonly called when his hide is on sale in a fur store, would make a fine pet if the wildness could be bred out of him and replaced with reliability. Smaller than a German Shepherd and closer to a Border Collie, the average mountain coyote weighs 9-11 kg. and stands about 50 cm. tall at the shoulder. The body may be 90 cm. long and carries a very bushy highly visible tail 35 cm. long. Coyotes are occasionally confused with the fox which shares the common characteristics of general appearance, sharp, pointed noses, keen eyes, and bushy tails. However, they are twice the size of most foxes and coloring tends to yellowish or tawny and grey.

Coyotes are primarily meat eaters but they have been known to enjoy a bit of a salad on the side. Some observers claim that coyotes eat anything that is edible and add variety with some things that are not. Rabbits and rodents are the main diet throughout the year, and larger animals such as deer or elk which are found dead or are occasionally successfully hunted, provide sporadic feasts. Coyotes at times team up to hunt the larger animals but are rarely successful unless the object of prey is in a weak condition and travelling conditions favor the coyotes. The flailing hooves of a deer,

elk or moose have often proven lethal to a coyote whose appetite was greater than its agility.

Examining coyote scats one usually finds wads of small animal hair and bone fragments mixed together with bits of feather, plant materials, and if close to town or a campground, miscellaneous pieces of garbage including chicken or pork bones and plastic bags. They are known to catch the odd fish, but do better catching frogs, tadpoles and crayfish. After missing a mouse coyotes might snack on a grasshopper or a low berry bush.

With the exception of acres of glacial ice and steep rocky slopes, coyotes can be found almost anywhere in the mountains. They are most common along the river valleys and lower slopes but can often be observed ranging above timberline 2255 m. in the proximity of grazing bighorn sheep and elk. Though they occasionally chase after the larger animals they are rarely successful and must depend on catching small rodents to feed themselves.

Accommodation for the average coyote is spartan. A hollow log, tiny cave of a simple den dug under the roots of a large tree or into a steep bank is usually sufficient. Sometimes an old burrow of a badger is merely enlarged and remodelled in order to minimize the overall ex-

Coyote Rick Kunelius

pense of labor involved. The final result is usually an entrance tunnel 30-60 cm. in diameter which may go back 1-9 m. Ambitious coyotes will have more than one shaft going back into the ground, while others will have the actual chamber close to the entrance. The living chamber at the end of the burrow may end up 133-1.5 m. below the ground surface. Bedding materials are brought in. Toilet functions are performed outside.

Coyotes are considered monogamous, sticking with the same mate on the same home range for life. They breed in late February or early March and about nine weeks later the mother may deliver five or six pups. Depending on overall health, the litter size may vary from a low of three to a high of twelve pups.

Shortly before the pups are born the male moves out and sets up temporary quarters nearby from which he will forage to find food for his mate and his new family. The new pups are blind for the first ten days but are soon outside frolicking and learning the ways of the real world. Their initial diet is milk and, later, partially digested food regurgitated by the parents.

Common enemies of the coyote include cougars, wolves, and eagles. Occasionally a bear will catch a coyote if it approaches too close to carrion which a bear may be feeding on. The sharp powerful hooves of elk, deer and moose are known to cripple or kill a coyote who boldly attacks and cannot get out of range in time.

Other enemies include common dog family diseases such as distemper, rabies and mange. Starvation is a common cause of death especially during winters of deep unsettled snow when the coyote flounders helplessly while larger animals pass only slightly hindered.

In the national parks where they are not hunted, most coyotes still remain wary of humans but the odd one with perhaps a more outgoing personality may come looking for handouts or entertainment. Once a coyote decides it is safe to play with people it is likely to hang around the same area, perhaps for the rest of its life. A coyote I called Old Charlie worked the Johnston Canyon, Hillsdale Meadow area and ranged over to the Eisenhower Rock across the river, entertaining visitors and taking whatever hand-outs were offered for at least five years till he finally disappeared. I often watched him hunting mice on the open meadows during the winter. He'd make a short

approach to the truck after I stopped just in case I had changed my ways and had a hand-out for him. Getting none he'd quickly turn back to hunting mice.

Generally there was sufficient snow crust to carry his weight and quietly he'd stalk across the surface sniffing and alternately turning his ear to the snow to listen. When he figured he had a fix on a mouse scurrying through its tunnel at the bottom of the snow pack, Charlie would reel back on his haunches and pounce, diving into the snow front paws together breaking the snow crust barely ahead of his delicate nose. Often his whole head would disappear to the shoulders and his back feet would scramble on the surface driving him deeper. It was only a second or two before he resurfaced, rarely with a mouse between his teeth. He seemed to know I was watching and would often throw a somewhat sheepish smile over his shoulder while stealthily moving off to the next pounce position.

When one realized how often a coyote comes up empty in his search for food it's no wonder they turn to easier ways to make a living.

Some coyotes, once established in a secure living, will turn to other pursuits. Old Charlie was known to steal children's toys from the nearby campground when he was well fed in the summertime. Another unnamed coyote became notorious for stealing golf balls off the far fairways on the Banff Springs Golf Course. He was tolerated for most of one summer until he had a run-in with a lady golfer who was not amused by his antics. Not about to lose her ball she put the chase on the coyote who in a moment of surprise dropped the ball. She retrieved the ball, turned and bent down to play it. Regaining his composure the coyote strode back to do battle for possession of the coveted ball and finding the lady with her back turned and bent over the ball, decided to divert her attention by first nipping her on the backside. This he did only to quickly discover that golf clubs can hit more than golf balls.

When the pups are about two months old the male is allowed to return home and together the parents take the pups out to teach them how to hunt and forage for food before they go off to establish their own territories. By late summer they are on their own, making a living and trying to avoid those animals which prey upon them as a food source.

DEER

Mule Deer and Fawn Byron Harmon, photo courtesy of the Whyte Foundation, Archives of the Canadian Rockies

HERE ARE TWO SPECIES of deer which range in the mountains, "mule deer" and "white-tail". They are quite similar in size and shape, and not only do their habits overlap but their habitats sometimes overlap as well.

Mule deer are a bit larger and stouter than white-tail. An average male stands about 1 m. tall at the shoulder and weighs 90-115 kg. They are 1.5 m. long. Females are noticeably smaller. Except during the late winter when the males shed their antlers, it is easy to distinguish between the two sexes since females do not grow antlers. Other than the size and antlers, within each species, the sexes look the same.

Mule deer have large mulish ears and grow antlers with tines that branch. During the winter they are a dark gray color but in the summer the top of the body is a yellowish brown and the undersides are darker brown. They have a large white patch on the rump and the 20 cm. tail is narrow and white with a black tip.

White-tail deer have smaller, more normal ears and grow antlers whose tines do not branch. The winter coat is gray or grayish brown. The summer coat is reddish brown with white undersides. The rump patch is not as obvious on the white-tail because the top of their broad and bushy tails match the upper body, effectively masking part of the rump. The hairy sides and bottom of the tail are white. When it is running, the tail is carried erect in the air, like a white flag waving good-bye.

Mule deer are jumpers and bounders while white-tail tend more to be runners. This simple difference in locomotion accounts for many of the differences between the species in selection of diet and habitat. Mule deer do well on steep hills and in downed timber while white-tails prefer more open and flatter river valley type ground with fewer obstacles.

In the past white-tail were very rare in the mountains but common out on the prairies and in the foothills where they are better adapted to travel. Over the past decade they have gradually pushed into the mountains sharing the broad river valleys with the mule deer. The upper slopes of the mountains still remain the exclusive domain of the mule deer.

Deer diets vary from location to location. In general they are primarily browsers but they do not turn down tender herbs and grasses, and will often spice up their menu with a good feed of mushrooms. Among the numerous types of leaves and twigs consumed by deer; willow, aspen, buffalo berry, saskatoon, gooseberry, and currant appear to be favorites, however, deer will apparently eat almost anything and some investigators have identified over 600 types of forage items when attempting to list out a deer diet in detail.

Deer range everywhere throughout the mountains, but they are more commonly seen at the lower elevations. Where white-tails tend to hang around the same range all their lives, mule deer will often travel large distances between winter and summer ranges. Winter finds them low in the valley bottoms but as the snow line recedes in spring they work their way up the mountainsides to near timberline. Males tend to range at higher elevations than the females.

Similar to elk and moose, home to a deer is wherever it happens to bed down. In the winter when the snow is deep they do not range far and though the beds are different each night, a particular thicket may be home for a while.

Breeding occurs during the fall and the rut is a rather quiet affair in comparison with the turmoil that goes on with elk. The males are polygamous and have no interest in their mates or their families once the breeding act is finished. Minor fighting occurs between males when more than one happens to choose a choice female at the same time. An enterprising buck may acquire a small harem of three or four does but the allurement lasts only a short time.

Generally a buck breeds with a doe and then goes off to see how many others it can do the same with before the season is over. After the rut the bucks settle down to the routine of winter, lose their antlers, and temporarily resemble the females.

When spring arrives the bucks grow antlers and the does bear young. Gestation lasts seven months and the fawns are born in June. They usually come out twins, each weighing 3 kg. Their eyes are open and their fawn colored coats are covered with white spots. When they are lying down hidden in a thicket, they resemble sun-splashed bumps in the forest. The fawns stay hidden in their nursery thickets for their first two weeks, only getting up when the doe returns from feeding to nurse them. Since the young fawns are so vulnerable to predators such as coyotes or bears their best survival strategy is to remain hidden until they gain sufficient strength and size to run with their mothers. By the time they are a month old they are well into eating green plants and running at speeds greater than 32 kph. They continue to nurse throughout the summer. The fawns travel with their mother and other families for the first year, until the doe drives them away to go off to bear her next set of twins.

Deer are subject to the same predators as the elk and moose but it is only rarely that healthy animals are caught. The most successful hunters are of course the cougar and wolves. Coyotes, bears, lynxes and wolverines may not be as efficient but they also obtain their share of succulent deer meat. Parasites and diseases such as nose worms, screw worms, and eye worms all help to weaken the deer, and if they do not actually cause death they result in the deer becoming easy prey for predators. Ticks are also common on deer and one can often see birds perched upon the backs of the deer picking out a meal of ticks.

Deer are considered to by shy and timid, yet they often adapt easily to the presence of people in situations where they are never hunted. The towns of Banff, Jasper and Waterton all have resident deer which wander through town with impunity. It is not that deer necessarily learn to like people, it is more that they inherently like the shrubs, flowers and gardens that people grow. The green thumbers of these towns learned long ago that to grow a successful garden or bed of flowers one first begins by building a strong wire fence. Fertilizer comes later.

ELK

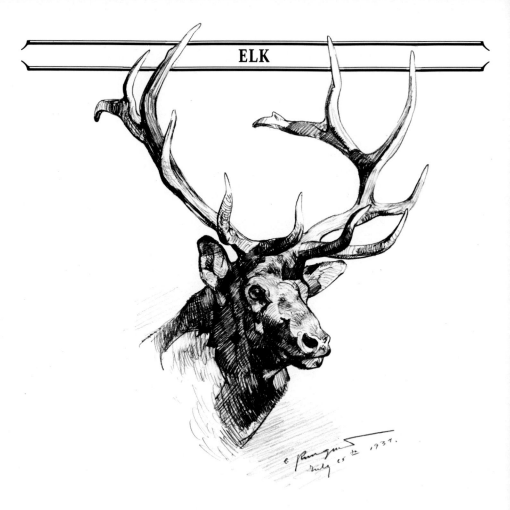

Bull Elk, Carl Rungius, (1869-1959), pencil sketch, courtesy of the Whyte Foundation, Peter Whyte Gallery

F ONE MOTORS ALONG the mountain highways in the early hours of dawn or late evening there is a good chance of spotting elk at almost any time during the year. These large, brown, deer-like animals almost rival the less common moose in size. An average male weighs 300-450 kg. He may grow to 2.5 m. in length and stand 1.5 m. tall at the shoulder. Their overall color is brownish-gray in summer and more of a yellowish-gray during the winter. They have a conspicuous large round tawny or whitish colored rump patch and a short 18 cm. tail. The females are 25% smaller than the males and are easily distinguished by their finer features and lack of antlers.

Each year the bulls grow massive, branching antlers which they shed in late winter. New antlers begin to grow when the first green vege-tation becomes available in the spring. As with moose and deer, the antlers are covered with a soft velvet-like tissue while they are growing. By late summer they reach full growth and the velvet dries up and is scraped off by rubbing against small trees. Elk cannot be aged by count-ing the number of branches on their antlers.

Elk do not have incisors (front teeth) in their upper jaw and cannot crop plants close to the ground the way that horses do. They were originally thought to be primarily grazers but recent research shows that they readily con-sume large amounts of browse material as well. Depending where the elk are, and perhaps how they feel, they will mix their diet between grass, flowers and twigs. Scars on the lower trunks of aspen trees were thought to be the result of starving elk eating bark in desperation,

Bull Elk Bruno Engler

however, elk just happen to like eating the odd bit of aspen and enjoy it even when their stomachs are full.

Elk range from the valley bottoms to timberline. Generally reluctant to expose themselves during the daylight hours, they take cover in the forests, coming out to graze in open meadows and avalanche paths when the sun goes down. Some elk live year-round in a small portion of a low river valley while others will migrate 60 km. between summer and winter pastures.

Home is wherever they happen to be at the end of the day's feeding. They will rarely bed down in the same spot twice and beds may be either a few metres or kilometres apart. Bulls range separately in small groups away from the cows and young except during the rutting season.

Elk have a dramatic breeding ritual which begins in late summer and may continue for two months. The larger bulls can be heard bugling and challenging each other for control of groups of cows throughout the fall. Each bull apparently tries to round-up as many cows as he can, but keeping control of them all is entirely another matter.

I once followed a bull with a harem of 26 cows on a September evening on the Banff Springs golf course. As they moved among the fairways other bulls would appear out of the forests and attempt to challenge the harem owner. One good bugle and a short rush with the massive antlers of the harem bull was usually enough to scare off the challengers. Amid the general confusion of challengers and other small groups of loose cow elk who were not part of the main harem, a young calf became separated from its mother. The calf was in the large herd and the mother off with another bull. The calf raised such a fuss at being separated from its mother that it drew the attention of the harem bull who finally decided he should perhaps retrieve that cow for himself as well as for the lamenting calf.

As soon as he left his own herd to chase down the cow in question two other bulls appeared from another direction and proceeded to split the harem, driving them off for their own purposes. It wasn't long before the original bull realized what had happened, and chasing his collected cow ahead of him, went thundering off into the woods after what used to be his group of cows.

It is generally assumed that the most powerful bulls do most of the breeding, but when one watches how much time and energy they expend keeping their harems together, it is hard to conceive how they would have enough energy left. Cows are only receptive for short periods and if the old master is not up to it, one of the young bulls is likely to slip in.

The gestation period is 8-9 months and the calves are born on low altitude ranges in late May and early June. Usually the cows find a secluded spot to bear their young, sometimes even seeking out islands in rivers. There are always exceptions to every rule and one cow was found to give birth just behind the horse corrals, a stone's throw from Banff townsite. Hardly a quiet remote location. The calves, generally single but sometimes twins, are reddish color with a white spotted coat. Their average weight at birth is 13 kg. The calf and mother stay apart from the others for two or three weeks until the calf is strong enough to travel with the herd. Once banded together again other cows will act as babysitters for short periods allowing the mother to get out for some fresh air and do some grazing on her own.

Occasionally in the summer, but more often in the fall after the breeding season, large herds of more than 100 animals can be seen.

An adult elk has few natural enemies but the young, old and infirm animals are subject to predation by wolves, cougars, bears and sometimes coyotes.

Bull Elk Al Williams for Banff National Park

Elk During Rutting Season, Carl Rungius, (1869-1959), etching on paper, courtesy of the Whyte Foundation, Peter Whyte Gallery

MOUNTAIN GOAT

THE MOUNTAIN GOAT IS not really a goat, it is most closely related to the old world antelope. To make matters worse it is often confused by casual observers with mountain sheep. For our purposes the goat is a goat. Adult billies weigh between 80-135 kg. though one would expect them to be much smaller under their coat of thick wool. In length they reach 1.5 m. with a 15 cm. tail. Shoulder height is about 1 m. Females are about 15% smaller but are otherwise almost indistinguishable from males. Both sexes have sharp black horns reaching 20-30 cm. in length. The sharp horns are effective puncture weapons and goats grow a thicker hide on the more exposed portions of their bodies. The skulls are quite fragile so goats rarely engage in butting behaviour common to sheep. Average age for a goat is 11 years.

Goats are completely covered with long white wooly fine hair which keeps them comfortable on the coldest, most exposed mountain tops. Their hooves are large and oval with a hard outer shell split down the middle, surrounding a soft cushion pad. The pads grip smooth rock while the outer shell and prominant dew claws provide good grip on terrain irregularities. Only with fancy mountaineering gear can man attempt to climb where goats so nimbly pass. Looking down calmly from a precarious ledge, on a high cliff band, with its white beard blowing in the wind, the goat has been likened to an old professor gazing vacantly overtop of his spectacles.

Because goats live in such inaccessible high mountain cliff habitat little is known about their feeding habits. Few other animals compete for their food sources since they are too much trouble and too dangerous to get to. They are known to eat grasses, flowers, alpine willow, mosses, lichens and the branches of alpine fir trees in varying quantities.

Though they usually range above 2000 m. they will often come down to valley bottoms during the summer to visit mineral licks. Goats range near and above timberline on alpine meadows, grassy slopes, cliff bands, scree and rock slides. They are rarely far away from broken cliff bands where they can easily flee to inaccessible ledges when danger threatens.

Home ranges are small, 24 sq. km. Summer ranges are larger and in a separate area from the winter range. Goats are somewhat sedentary, rarely inclined to move any distance without good reason. Adult males spend most of their time by themselves or in small groups of half a dozen or fewer. Females and immatures are quite sociable and have been sighted in mid-summer bands of 50-60 animals. Often, they will range in the same area as bighorn sheep but tend to be just above the sheep and closer to the cliff bands. There is hardly a high mountain within the national parks which does not have goat on it at some time during the year.

Home to a goat is anyplace which is inaccessible to most other animals as long as there is food available along the ledges.

Goats rut in November. The gestation period is about six months and single kids are born in late spring. Within a few minutes of birth the kid is able to stand up and reach for its first feeding from nanny standing overtop. At birth kids weigh about 3 kg. and stand 33 cm. tall. Within an hour or so the kid is able to begin hobbling about in a confined area carefully watched by its nanny.

Kids continue to nurse throughout the summer, gradually building up their ability to identify and consume adult goat foods. They remain in close association with the mother goat for their first year until it is time for the next generation to be born.

Although goats are generally well protected by the natural fortresses in which they live, the young of the year must keep a sharp eye open skyward to avoid the dive of a strong determined eagle. Away from their protective cliffs all goats must be aware of bears, cougars, wolves and coyotes which might cut off their retreat paths and close in for the kill.

Similar to the other big game animals goats are plagued with numerous ailments including pneumonia, tape worms, stomach worms and tick infestations.

Rock slides take a small toll on goats but the greatest danger is winter snow avalanches. Goats literally live within and around the starting zones and accumulation basins of the avalanches. In the summer while walking the bases of avalanche fans one can sometimes find

The Goat House in the Banff Animal Paddock, photo courtesy of the Whyte Foundation, Archives of the Canadian Rockies

the remains of goats and sheep caught unaware during the winter.

Goats sometime get careless when they think they are in an area devoid of predators such as in remote alpine meadows surrounded by glaciers and cliff bands. I once found the carcass of an adult goat caught by a grizzly bear in the middle of the Niverville Meadows remotely located in the Freshfield Icefields. The only access route I could find imaginable for the bear was to have worked its way over 2.5 km. of glacier ice. A bear would appear there so rarely that the goats likely had no thought of danger.

It is hard to think of goats being similar to red squirrels but they do share a couple of surprising similarities. Both are good swimmers and can easily cross lakes and long coastal inlets. If a goat is climbing along a narrow rock ledge which gradually peters out to a sheer rock face without room to turn around, it can calmly rear up on its front legs, keeping its weight against the cliff, and walk its back end around above itself to complete the turn of direction. While in mid-turn the goat (from a distance) resembles a squirrel scampering down a tree trunk.

MARMOT

THE HOARY MARMOT OCCUPIES a special place in the hearts of many matronly mountain hikers. Regardless of the observer's age, marmots always seem to exude a captivating, charming appeal. Marmots are small, weighing only 7 kg. as adults. Their 52 cm. body carries a full bushy tail of an additional 23 cm. A large marmot stands 18 cm. at the shoulder. Females are smaller than males but to the average human observer they are indistinguishable. Color is quite variable but in general they are a mixture of black and white often tinged with rust, and a buff red on the hind quarters. On their feet they appear to wear blackish brown boots.

If marmots are not out sunning themselves on warm rocks, they always appear to be eating. When it is stormy they stay underground. They eat grasses, herbs, flowering plants, roots and berries. They eat and grow fat for the very good reason that they do not enjoy winter and are clever enough to sleep right through it. One rarely sees a marmot beyond late September.

They emerge from their grass lined chambers among fields of boulders in late April or in some cases not until late May, when they can be assured of decent weather and a diet of fresh vegetation. Time of emergence coincides with the new spring plant growth. Those living in lower rock slopes of the eastern valleys will naturally be out earlier than their relatives in the rocks higher up or farther west.

They hibernate for three-quarters of the year and don't need to rush around gathering quantities of food to store for winter. Marmots are quite content to live leisurely in a small area so long as the boulders are large enough to allow them easy passage underneath for protection and for the location of sleeping chambers. They are not noted as diggers or creatures who expend much energy in building homes.

The parents mate shortly after coming out of hibernation and four or five young are born about a month later. Very similar to their close relatives, the woodchucks, baby marmots are tiny, blind, naked, pink little things about 10 cm. long weighing barely 40 gm. They are nursed for a month until their eyes open and a reasonable coat of hair is grown. Then they venture up to the outside world of green plants.

The toilet-training process is ponderously slow for the mother marmot who must continuously haul out the soiled grass bedding and bring in fresh material until the young can venture outside.

Once out and about the young are only tolerated in the home residence until mid-summer when they are encouraged to set up separate residences nearby. In the fall they wander off to find territories of their own.

Marmots (in French, Siffleur) are the whistlers of the animal world. They do not purse their lips as they merrily whistle away but rather the sound is formed in the throat with a full diaphragm of air to force it out. They can often be heard over 1 km. away.

The whistling is not only sociable, it is also an extremely effective warning system. When danger threatens and the warning blast is blown, not only do all the other marmots heed the warning but every other animal in the vicinity seems to pay attention. Birds stop singing, ground squirrels and pikas head for cover and even larger mammals raise their heads and take time to look around. The warning may pass across entire hillsides as other marmots continue the alarm.

Marmots have always been prized by Europeans and Indians alike for their delectable meat. Eagles, hawks, coyotes, lynx, cougars, wolves and bears all seem to agree that it's hard to beat a good marmot for lunch. Being so highly prized by so many predators it is probably a very wise move on the part of the marmot to only expose itself for a few months of the year.

Hoary Marmot Carole Harmon

MOOSE

Moose, Carl Rungius, (1869-1959), etching on paper, courtesy of the Whyte Foundation, Peter Whyte Gallery

ALE MOOSE ARE THE LARGEST antlered animals on earth. The weight range varies between 360 kg. and 635 kgs. and they are commonly up to 2 m. tall at the shoulder. They may grow to 3 m. in length but their tail is a mere 12 cm. long. Moose are usually an overall dark color made up of mixtures of brown and black though they may have lighter patches and a somewhat grizzled appearance. White or albino moose occur rarely. The young are reddish brown and do not have the spots which are so characteristic of young deer.

Females are smaller than males and are easily distinguished because they do not grow antlers. The males grow large, palmate antlers which do not reach full size until the moose are four years old. Each winter the males shed their antlers, then begin to grow a new set in the spring.

After the antlers are dropped it can be difficult to distinguish the two sexes until the new antler buds begin to show. While the antlers are growing they are covered with a soft tissue layer of velvet. Under the expanding velvet there is an extensive vascular system which provides the nutrients for antler growth. By the end of the summer the antlers reach full development and the velvet covering dries up and is gradually shed to reveal hard, white antlers which change color to brown with use. Large males may grow antlers which spread 125-180 cm. Both sexes have a strange upside down, bell-shaped sack which hangs from their bottom jaw and may be 15-25 cm. long. It has no known useful purpose, it just hangs around. Similar to elk and deer, moose do not have front teeth (incisors) on their upper jaws.

Moose are quite particular about their diet

and prefer succulent aquatic plants and the new growth ends of branches from shrubs. Because their legs are so long they do not graze well at ground levels and prefer taller plants such as ferns and fireweed, usually nipping off the tender ends. They are strong swimmers but only feed on aquatic plants when they can stand comfortably in the shallows. The most delightful moments of moose watching occur when one finds a big bull feeding in the shallows. After he consumes the easily accessible surface vegetation he thinks nothing of plunging his whole head under the surface to grasp the underwater plants. When his head reappears the antlers often are unceremoniously draped with all manner of vegetable material. It's the worst job of temporary decorating ever conceived, but hardly embarassed, he does it again and again.

Even in summer, when soft green plants are readily available, moose will often switch to browsing on the hardier shrubs which sustain them through the winter. Favorite browse species include aspen, willow, birch and even the coniferous fir tree. If a moose can't reach up to the branches it wants it will often walk down the whole tree bending it over with the weight of its massive chest.

Moose fare best in forests which are at their early successional stages. Areas of regrowth after a fire or after logging are favored moose habitat. Few moose can be found in the mountains where forest fires have been suppressed and logging activity is not permitted. In these areas they often depend on avalanches to keep the vegetation at a successional stage.

Moose range from valley bottom lakes to near timberline in their search for food, but they generally avoid tall, mature forests. They seem to love dense willow and will spend weeks at a time in their favorite thickets. Although they have long powerful legs and are hardly hindered by deep snows, they do not range over any great distance. Moose range may be as small as 5-10 sq.km.

Moose are not very sociable animals. They spend most of their time wandering alone. In the winter they may yard-up in small groups of up to six animals for a brief conference before going their separate ways again.

The rut, or mating time, occurs in the fall, generally October-November when the animals are at their strongest and the bulls proudly strut their full grown polished antlers. At this time males will wander beyond their usual range to find an accommodating female to spend a brief period with. Seemingly quickly bored with intimate relationships, strong bulls may manage numerous affairs before the breeding season is over.

As early summer approaches, previously patient mothers tire of their one or two yearling calves which they have educated and traveled with for the previous year and drive them away before going off to a secluded spot to bear new offspring. Pregnant for eight months, mother moose get very little time away from raising young which is generally an annual affair.

Cows usually give birth to two calves. They are gangly legged miniature caricatures of their mothers. A calf weighs about 11-13 kg. After lying down and nursing for a few days they can stand fairly securely by the fourth day. At two weeks the young are learning to seek out and chew easily digested plants. They grow rapidly over the first summer but do not attain adult size for about three years. They are protected by the female for the first year and may even become re-united for a short period after the female bears and establishes her new young of the following year.

Wolves and cougars are the enemy of the moose. They are most susceptible to these carnivores when they are young, or when heavy snow crusts support the weight of the predators but not the moose. Wolves hunting in packs take the greatest toll. Bears are known to kill young calves and have been seen to attack adult moose on rare occasions. The massive strength of a healthy moose and their lightning fast hooves drive all but the most determined bears away. Healthy adult moose fear few enemies.

Though not considered a predator, ticks can have a significant effect on weakening moose and making them easier prey for wolves and cougars. These tiny insects attach themselves everywhere on a moose and proceed to draw blood until they are fully engorged at which time they simply fall off. Originally only a 2 mm. long speck of an insect they slowly grow to the size of the last joint on your little finger as they fill themselves with blood. Some researchers have estimated that a moose may be infected with over 10,000 ticks at one time.

A peculiar cause of death occurs when moose are in association with white-tailed deer. The deer carry a parasite which, though it does not affect deer causes brain disease in moose. The

Bull Moose Bruno Engler

parasite invades the brain causing lack of co-ordination, lameness, blindness and eventually paralysis and death. Luckily, white-tailed deer do not generally favor mountainous terrain and moose in the Canadian Rockies are not bothered with this strange disease.

Though there are always exceptions, moose do their best to avoid humans, and it is best that humans should not attempt to get too close to them. A female protecting newly born will put the run on anyone who ventures too near.

When Banff was a quiet little town in the late forties a peculiar old bull moose wandered into town one fall and discovered tantalizing left-overs in back lane garbage cans. Initially a curiousity and a bit of a spectacle, the old bull was tolerated until he went too far in attempting to communicate with the town school children. Most likely the kids had a part in tormenting him by throwing things and dashing about, which was acceptable until the moose began chasing the kids. By the time the situation reached the newspaper the story came out with headlines claiming moose threatens children on way home from school. Needless to say the old fellow was summarily charged, convicted and dispatched to greener pastures.

PIKA

IKA (PRONOUNCED "PEEKA") resemble guinea pigs. If you stretch them out you might get 18 cm. in length but in their normal posture they look to be only 7-10 cm. long. Their little 1.5 cm. tail is barely noticeable. Weighing only 15 gm. one would almost expect them to be blown away in a strong wind. They change their coats twice a year and when usually seen are an overall gray color tinged with buff and a few blackish guard hairs. Even the bottoms of their feet are covered with hair, as might be expected of this smallest member of the hare family.

Pika H.U. Green

Unlike rabbits, their back legs are not much longer than their front legs so they do not bound, but rather hop lightly about. They are not known to sit up on their hind legs like their larger relatives. Only pikas can distinguish males from females.

Pikas are the little farmers of the mountains. They do not hibernate and they do not tunnel well through snow, so they must put up sufficient stacks of hay in their underground barns to see themselves through the winter.

They consume a wide variety of plants. Examined hay stacks have included numerous types of grasses, sedges, fireweed, aster, goldenrod, heather, yarrow, flox, ferns, aspen leaves, cinquefoil, raspberry, rose, saskatoon, gooseberry and various other plants.

These little harvesters momentarily abandon the safety of their rocks to rush about clipping and gathering favorite plants. They carry their harvest bundles crossways in their mouths. After their first bite the bundle resembles a set of overlarge whiskers sticking out from both cheeks. By the time they head back to the rocks they are carrying a bundle almost as big as themselves. The bundles are carefully spread out in the sun to dry before being added to the growing haystacks.

The pika works during the day but manages to find ample time to take regular siestas. The middle hours of the day are often spent perched on a warm sloping rock soaking up the rays and chatting with neighbors or taking turns on the colony watch for intruders.

Pikas are found on rock slides between the 1800-2500 m. level throughout the mountains. Being so small they are difficult to locate except by following up their sharp, short peeking whistle. Since they are somewhat adept at ventriloquism one must stop and remain still while scanning the rocks not just where the sound seemd to come from but throughout the general area as well. Soon a tiny furry rock will come to life in front of ones' eyes just before disappearing behind a bigger non-animate rock.

They do not require a large territory and some colonies have been estimated at six pikas an acre. Because their homes are deep within the bouldery confusion of rock slides it is difficult to obtain information concerning their domestic affairs.

It seems that the young are born at various times throughout the spring and summer probably only weighing 9 gm. at birth. Brood sizes varies from three to five youngsters. They are cared for and kept underground by the parents until they are about three-quarters grown. By the following spring they are definitely out farming on their own.

If a pika can make it safely into the rocks it is generally safe from most predators with the exception of weasels and martens which carry on the chase underground. During the day watch must be kept for foxes, coyotes, wolverines, hawks and eagles. Occasionally a large bear will make an initial attempt to dig out a little pika, but the energy expended can hardly be worth the reward if it is persistent enough to actually catch one. Other population limiting factors are disease, stomach worms, tape worms and fleas. Fleas are not much of a problem to larger animals but to an animal as small as a pika they are probably the equivalent of horseflies to people.

PORCUPINE

UST BECAUSE PORCUPINES ARE slow moving creatures who carry a fully effective defence network of quills, there is no reason to assume, as many people do, that they are dumb or slow witted. Porcupine watchers have discovered that they are adaptable and can learn to master a maze much faster than many acknowledged "intelligent" animals. Porcupines can even become affectionate and interesting pets, but never cuddly.

They are probably considered dumb because they move so ponderously and have rather poor eyesight. The fact that they do not hibernate also leads one to question their intelligence.

The average porcupine is 83 cm. long including its 18 cm. tail. They stand about 30 cm. tall at the shoulder and weigh 9-11 kg. Generally they are black or dark brown with some ivory or yellow tipped hairs. They have a heavy, high arched body and short bowed legs. And of course, their most distinguishing feature is their quills.

The entire body with the exception of the underbody and feet is covered with quills of various lengths. On the cheeks they are less than 1 cm., on the back about 5 cm., and on the rump and tail up to 6 cm. Quills are continually growing, molting and being lost in encounters with objects and other animals. Though I know of no one who has actually counted the number of quills on a porcupine, I would venture to guess they carry 20,000 to 30,000 of them.

The quills are not simply hollow spears with fish hook type barbs on the end. Hollow they are, but the outer black tips are covered with dozens of minute barbs overlapping each other like scales on a fish. They do not "shoot" their quills. At the body end the quill is connected lightly to a muscle lying just under the skin. This muscle sheet controls the direction of the quills and also allows them to be released and pulled away with the greatest of ease. When another animal runs into a porcupine the barbed ends of the quills pierce the skin of the intruder while the muscle holding the quill relaxes and releases the other end. Whoever walks away from a porcupine encounter carries a souvenir of the intensity of their own initial antagonism. The porcupine was merely there and bears no ill feelings to anyone.

Porcupine Carole Harmon

Differentiating between the sexes is only of concern to porcupines, for no one is his right mind is likely to lift the tail to find out.

Porcupines are vegetarians specializing in consuming the cambium (inner bark) layers of numerous trees as their staple food. During the summer when green forage is abundant they consume a variety of plant leaves including currants, gooseberry, buffalo berry, and rose, as well as grass, aster, lupine, cinquefoil and dandelion to name a few. Besides the inner bark of the coniferous trees they often eat the tender needles of the previous year's growth. Often porcupines end up killing trees in their slow enthusiasm to consume the inner bark. Rather than working up one side only they will completely girdle a tree, thereby cutting off its supply of nutrients. In the perspective of the overall forest the loss is rarely significant.

Porcupines are also extremely fond of bones and shed antlers. These possibly serve a dual purpose of honing their teeth as well as supplying essential mineral nutrients to their bodies. Similar to people, porcupines have obsessions. Their greatest food obsession is salt. They will chew anything with salt on it–axe handles, clothing with traces of salty perspiration, rims of toilet seats, saddles and leather rigging to name but a few common camp articles. Their second great obsession appears to be the glue used in plywood. Anyone foolish enough to build with plywood in porcupine country will soon find windows which were never part of the original architectural plans. Even plywood signs on steel posts are not immune if the snow-pack happens to approach the height of the sign.

Being slow, porcupines do not range far afield but their range includes the third dimension since they do spend a significant amount of time up in the trees. Though individually they do not travel far they can be found anywhere from the edges of desert areas to timberline in the mountains. Their own personal range may be confined within an acre for an entire season, then they might actually waddle several miles between low elevation winter ranges and higher summer ranges. Their travel trails are not beaten into the earth but may sometimes be located by following the porcupine blazes upon the trees.

Water is no obstacle to a porcupine since its dense inner coat of hair traps air and each quill is hollow and filled with air. They are naturally buoyant but are not great paddlers.

Porcupines are not considered to be sociable animals, and normally they eat and travel alone. However they are not averse to sharing a delectable area with others, in fact they often "den" together. Home is nothing fancy; a hollow log, stump, brushpile, thicket, or even an opening under a tumble of rocks. Homes are only occupied during the winter and when bearing young. Dens are often marked by great piles of small porcupine pellets just outside their entrance.

How porcupines mate has long been a matter of strange conjecture around many campfires. As it turns out the conception is far from immaculate but it is definitely impeccably accurate and at the mutual consent of both parties. The female normally makes the first advance. They mate like other animals, the female is able to pull her quills down tightly against her body, or allow them to lie so limply that she avoids wounding the male.

Porcupines mate in the fall and the gestation period is a full seven months long. They bear only one offspring in their humble dens. The babies are about 30 cm. long from nose to tip of tail, weigh close to 0.45 kg. and are heavily clothed in long black hair and a full set of quills. Their eyes are already open and their teeth are well on the way to full development.

The quills are not a problem at birth because the young porcupines are born inside a membranous sac. It is not until they are torn out of their delivery sac and the quills dry in the outside air that they become hard and effective.

For the first week young porkies are raised on milk before graduating to lush green plant materials. Affection between mother and offspring is necessarily limited to nose rubs and grunts of endearment. From its second day the young porcupine can climb and amble about quite successfully. In fact, on its very first day, though not capable of travel, it displays inherent defence reactions. The first six months are spent following the mother around, eating and sleeping curled up on the ground. By fall the young porcupine is almost half grown and wanders off to live its own life.

Porcupines have few natural enemies. Only the fisher is known to be proficient at attacking porcupines on their vulnerable undersides. The fox, lynx, wolverine, and cougar are occasional successful predators. Wolves, coyotes and bears can also be added to the list of animals that porcupines would rather not encounter.

Common with other wildlife, porkies are susceptible to the insidious tiny enemies of the body which include tapeworms, roundworms, threadworms, ticks and lice. Forest fires also easily over-run these slow moving creatures.

Porcupines are somewhat akin to people in their range of individual personalities. Some are serious and some are frivolous. Young animals play together when they encounter each other; wrestling, biting, grunting and defending themselves from imaginary enemies. Even an adult porcupine dances. He'll stand up on his hind feet with his tail splayed out for extra balance and proceed to rock and roll, throwing his weight onto one foot while raising the other, then switching and rolling his weight to the other foot. Head and shoulders swing naturally from side to side and the arms often punch out aimlessly in front. It's not far off from the dance styles of the seventies.

Bighorn Rams Sparring Rick Kunelius

BIGHORN SHEEP

Bighorn Rams Rick Kunelius

SLIGHTLY AHEAD OF THE Columbian ground squirrel, the bighorn sheep rates as the most popular animal of the visitors to the Canadian Rockies. The adult rams with their massive curling horns are among the most highly prized trophy heads available on the North American continent, outside of the National Parks of course. Best of all, sheep are just plain friendly and seeable during most of the year. They range low in the Athabasca valley near Jasper townsite, along the highway just north of the Columbia Icefields, and along the road again above the Vermillion Lakes near Banff. Though large rams are seldom seen on top of Sulphur Mountain it is a rare day that a band of sheep does not appear near the upper terminal of the gondola lift. Sometimes it seems that they are simply there waiting to get their pictures taken.

The hollow haired coat of the bighorn sheep varies in color from grayish-brown, light brown, to dark brown. A short, darker tail is outlined by a large white rump patch and a band of white trim outlines the backs of all four legs. Sheep are almost human in size, adult rams weighing 70-115 kg. and females 50-75 kg. Adult rams in length reach 1.5 m. and stand 1 m. high at the shoulder. Ewes are about 15% smaller. It is easy to distinguish adult males from the other sheep by their massive curling horns which develop to form a full circle. These horns grow as large as 111 cm. in circumference with a base circumference of 40 cm. The combined weight of a dried skull and horns can easily exceed 11 kg.

Both males and females grow horns but those of the female are very thin and rarely exceed 25 cm. An adult female looks very similar to a young male until the horn growth of the male begins to exceed the standard female length when he is past two years old. Since females and juveniles range together it can be quite confusing, trying to tell them apart in the field. The way sheep carry-on at times, it seems that the sheep don't care if they can separate the sexes themselves either. Very few Bighorn live beyond 12 or 14 years of age.

Sheep consume a wide variety of grasses, forbs and sedges. In the spring and early summer they are strongly attracted to mineral licks and will travel long distances to satisfy their cravings. The minerals found in the licks may be very important for horn and bone development.

Bighorn sheep have distinct summer and winter ranges which, depending on local circumstance, may be close together or far apart. They are not well adapted for pawing through deep snow and they select for their winter range slopes which are exposed to the sun and blown relatively free of snow. The ideal range is one which has steep grassy slopes with cliff bands nearby to which they can flee for safety if danger threatens. Except for the large rams they are not adapted for fighting and they must depend upon their natural skills as mountain climbers to avoid predators.

Sheep rarely travel alone, females and immatures band together and rams form bachelor groups on separate ranges. They feed early in the morning, rest during mid-day and feed again through the evening. Home is wherever they scoop out a comfortable depression to lay in. When resting there are always one or two who act as sentries for the safety of the band.

Like the elk, sheep have a very dramatic breeding ritual but they do not bugle as the elk do. The rut begins in the late fall when the rams move onto the same ranges as the females and young. Long before the first female is mounted the rams have already established who gets first choice. Their massive horns are not just decoration to allure the opposite sex, they are also extremely effective battering rams which establish who is king of the castle among the rams. They literally go about banging their heads together as hard as they can to determine who is the toughest and consequently the leader. To the victor go the spoils!

There is no sense of decency in a sheep herd during the rut. Small rams practise on each other and the larger rams continually challenge the victors, probably hoping to ultimately beat them down through team effort. Since the commanding rams do not attempt to drive their harems off to seclusion, in the manner which elk attempt, there is always a good chance for a

Bighorn Ram Bruno Engler

smaller ram to slip in unnoticed to attempt a quick breeding act on a receptive female. But woe to the smaller ram if the master catches him in the act, he might likely butt him off toward the stars.

The gestation period is about six months and young individual lambs are born in May and June. At birth they weight 3.5-4.5 kg. and stand almost 45 cm. tall at the shoulder. For the first few weeks they have to reach to suckle but by the end of six months they are already two-thirds the height of their mothers.

Although sheep are subject to predation by wolves, coyotes, cougars, lynx, wolverines, bears and eagles, none of the above animals have a significant effect on sheep populations. Their exceptional eyesight, awareness and climbing ability usually enable them to avoid trouble. They are most vulnerable when young or when far away from escape terrain such as at an inconvenient mineral lick. Natural physical hazards such as winter avalanches take a small but regular toll of sheep.

When sheep ranges become overpopulated the sheep do not disperse naturally. Historic catastrophic die-offs have occured through pneumonia lungworm disease which has the effect of stabilizing sheep populations in North America.

COLUMBIAN GROUND SQUIRREL

BSERVING THE GROUND SQUIRREL meadow at the entrance to the buffalo enclosure near Banff townsite, I have come to the conclusion that people are more interested in these cheeky little rodents than the buffalo. Visitors seem to spend more time being entertained by the ground squirrels, and trying to entertain them, than they do observing the massive brutes in the paddock.

Columbian ground squirrels are among the largest of the various ground squirrel species. They are one-third larger than their cousins the common gopher, of the prairies to the east. They have short ears, tails, and legs but their little legs are well adapted for burrowing. Columbians measure about 35 cm. in length which includes their 10 cm. tail. They stand about 7.5 cm. tall at the shoulder and weigh only 565 gm. They are a mixture of colors though commonly a mottled rusty gray with tones of yellow. Though at the opposite end of the size spectrum from the grizzly bears, they also have grizzled (whittish-tipped) hairs mixed through their coats. The undersides tend to be more tawny or rusty yellow.

Their appetite is inexhaustible and understandably so since they must consume enough in four months to fatten-up for eight months of hibernation. Similar to the marmots they do not stay awake to experience Indian Summer during the fall but rather disappear underground at the end of summer.

Most of the food they manage to store in their underground chambers is not consumed until the following spring when they can lay back in bed and happily munch away until the weather improves and the plants are sufficiently succulent to warrant going outside.

Ground squirrels eat a wide variety of leaves and stems of numerous grasses and herbs. They also consume the flowers of dandelions and buttercups, and the bulbs of wild onions, glacier lilies and camas. When the berries ripen they happily devour almost any berry within reach. As the vegetation dries out and goes to seed, all available seeds are either immediately eaten, or stored for spring consumption. Judging from their interaction with people it also appears that if available they will accept peanuts, sunflower seeds, popcorn, gum drops, jelly beans, potato chips and kleenex. (The latter is more likely used for soft bedding material.)

The range of a Columbian ground squirrel is rather limited to the immediate vicinity of the burrow area. It is not uncommon to find six ground squirrels to the acre. Colonies might spread for miles but individual animals do not range far from home. Though limited in their own individual travel, through diversity in numbers, Columbian ground squirrels are the most common and widespread mammal in the mountains. They are everywhere from low river valleys to high alpine meadows.

Their season of activity relates directly to the location of the home range. The lowland animals surface earlier than their alpine neighbors and retire earlier at the end of summer. The alpine ground squirrels do not stay out later out of choice but rather as a function of putting on the requisite fat to survive hibernation. Getting a slow start, it takes them longer to finish.

Home is a simple yet complicated affair. The actual sleeping and hibernating chamber is a

Columbian Ground Squirrel Bob Sandford

plain spherical cell about 23 cm. in diameter, located at the end of one of many tunnels, 0.6-0.9 m. below ground level. The other tunnels serve as passageways, storage areas and moisture drainage channels. All of the dirt excavated in burrowing is laboriously pushed up to the surface through one outlet. After the hibernating chamber is established a partial exit is dug out prior to the long winter sleep. When the ground squirrels awaken in the spring they burrow out the remainder of this tunnel to the outside world through their old last year burrow entrance.

Additional tunnels are created, possibly to confuse the enemy should a weasel or other small predator follow them into the underground chambers. Some tunnel systems in total add up to 20 m. for one animal! Many passages apparently go nowhere but their terminus is not far from the surface in case a hurried exit is required. They are not opened ahead of time in order to keep them secret.

When the little guys give up on summer and go down to hibernate, usually in late August, they disappear into their sleeping cells and plug off the entrance to the cell with loose dirt tamped into place with their nose. They curl-up into a tight little ball, drop their body temperature by half and disappear into a comatose stupor until spring.

A week or so after coming out of hibernation they begin to breed. Normally careful and watchful for predators, caution is thrown to the wind in their rush to find an appropriate partner. Once mating is completed, order is restored and males and females go back about their orderly cautious business of making a living.

The gestation period is just under four weeks and the young are born in a special nursery cell underground. Litter sizes average about seven naked, blind, toothless little creatures weighing only 14 gm. They develop rapidly and in two weeks are already five times heavier. After three weeks of nursing, their eyes open and their bodies are covered with light fur. Gradually they venture up to the surface and by the time they are six weeks old they are ready to set-up their own home quarters.

Within three months the little ground squirrels are not only born and raised but they have put on enough fat to survive the first hibernation period in their own makeshift homes.

Almost every flesh-eating animal is a potential predator to the innocent ground squirrels.

The most common diners upon ground squirrels include hawks, eagles, coyotes, foxes, wolves, bears, wolverines and badgers. No wonder they go out of their way to dig extra tunnels and rapid-exit burrows!

I will never forget the day one summer afternoon when I happened to be in the Banff warden office and a distraught tourist walked in requesting a shovel. He had walked over from the meadow by the buffalo paddocks where he had been required to abandon his car. We've had a lot of strange requests but no one before had ever come in asking for a shovel in the summer time. It hadn't snowed for weeks. As it turned out his family had been playing with the ground squirrels and the kids had used up all the peanuts and potato chips before dad could get a good picture of his little son with the ground squirrels. Out of edibles, he reasoned that the next best attraction would be something that glitters. The first thing that came to mind was the car keys. So his three-year-old son tottered into the midst of the ground squirrels dangling the car keys. The perfect photographic moment presented itself with an adult ground squirrel standing-up on its hind legs to investigate the glittering keys held by little Johnny. In the excitement of the moment when the shutter snapped Johnny released his grip on the keys and the ground squirrel, true to form, grabbed the keys and disappeared down the hole. Knowing the ground was dry and hard and that he wouldn't cause much damage, nor expose more than one per cent of the burrow, we passed him a shovel while someone else in another room quietly called the locksmith.

RED SQUIRREL

Red Squirrel H.U. Green

ONSIDERING ITS TINY SIZE the red squirrel is outstanding in its ability to make itself known to all intruders who may venture through its forest domain. Some people even compare them to an angry alarm clock going off before sunrise. The nickname "chickaree" only begins to express the racous stacatto sounds which come endlessly from these little forest creatures when they are disturbed or merely talking to themselves. Weighing in at a mere 225 gm. one would hardly consider them a worthy challenger. They stretch out to 30-35 cm. in length which includes a 12 cm. bushy tail. Height at the shoulder is a proud 9 cm.

As their names implies, they are a rusty red color overall with a whitish underbelly separated by a dark line running along the flank on both sides. It is difficult to distinguish males from females unless you are a squirrel yourself.

Red squirrels are voracious eaters and though they appear to concentrate on coniferous cones they happily consume a wide variety of materials including nuts and the fruits and seeds of strawberries, currants, juniper, gooseberry and any other berry. Mushrooms are picked and set out to dry before going into winter storage. Insects are plucked from under loose tree bark and any available larvae are happily snatched up for immediate consumption. Old bones and shed antlers, though hardly appetizing, are chewed regularly and appear to be an important part of dental hygiene and a probable source of phosphorous and calcium. Squirrels are known to eat bird eggs and small fledglings but these are more dietary exceptions than the rules.

The home range of a red squirrel is easily encompassed in a diameter of 150-200 m., but one must visualize the vertical dimension to the tops of the trees as well. Within this range it will establish numerous food storage caches and at least one major "midden." These are central areas used repeatedly for husking the cones of spruce and pine to gain access to the interior seed. Over the years these heaps may grow to be 3 m. across and almost 1 m. high. Within the midden heap numerous tunnels link storage vaults and it is not uncommon for a squirrel to put up an annual crop of five bushels of cones within one midden. Since larger animals often capitalize upon red squirrel food caches it is important that they diversify their assets in as many places as they can within accessible range.

Winter is a time of leisure when an ample food supply has been stored and there is no need to venture out on stormy days. Burrows under the snow connect various food caches but on sunny days the red squirrel seems to prefer scampering about outside and digging up prized caches.

The home of the red squirrel appears in a variety of forms. It may be carefully constructed of twigs, leaves and moss, or it may be a simple burrow into the ground under the base of a tree, or a high rise suite in an abandoned woodpecker hole, or in a hollow tree. The nest room averages 20 cm. in diamter with about 12 cm. ceiling height. Soft materials line the inside. Though squirrels do not foul their own nests they are sloppy housekeepers and are often over-run with fleas and mites. When the fleas get out of control or an enemy gets too close, there is always an extra home or two or three already built within the home into which the squirrel quickly moves.

Red squirrels always seem to be chasing about together and playing sociably, but in fact they are rather solitary creatures. They pair up in late winter and spring and mating continues through March and April. The gestation period lasts about six weeks and the young are born blind and naked, similar to mice. The average litter is five or six. Within ten days the young grow a sufficient coat of fur to be presentable but they continue to nurse until they are five to seven weeks old. By then they are one-third grown and begin to venture out into the world. Most families are scattered by fall but late broods may stay together until early the following spring.

Families are large and squirrels breed annually, but the overall population is kept in check by numerous natural predators. Most red squirrels are lucky to live more than five years. Common enemies include the blood thirsty pine marten, weasel, mink, coyote, and lynx. A sharp eye also has to be kept open for hawks. If a squirrel ventures out at night, the ever present owls are quick to claim him. Seed crop failures and raided food caches may result in simple starvation.

Surprisingly, red squirrels are good swimmers and think little of crossing even wide, fast flowing rivers. I've heard it said that a squirrel was seen to paddle several miles across a lake! Water adventures hold other hazards such as low swooping gulls from above, and large fish attacking from below.

Squirrels are fascinating little creatures to watch as they bound about at high speeds, jumping from branch to branch, galloping across the ground and tearing unconcerned up and down the tree trunks. They can jump 2 m. from branch to branch and can usually recover a failed landing by righting themselves and catching a branch below. Speeding down a vertical tree trunk, they seem to go unchecked by gravity. In fact they are in full control placing one foot at a time in a kind of a trot, reversing their back feet to act as brakes.

WOLF

Wolf Bruno Engler

OLVES HAVE HAD A HARD TIME in the Canadian Rockies over the past century. Man has enjoyed a one-sided vendetta with the wolf, and even in the National Parks they were not safe until recently. The estimated population in Banff Park, (4000 km.) was a mere 38 wolves in 1950. In 1952-53 a wolf control operation was carried out in connection with a rabies control program. So successful was it that in 1953 the population was estimated at four survivors. Since that time wolves have been left alone in the National Park and are making a slow comeback. The wolf population would grow faster but for their bad habit of wandering out to provincial lands where they still get shot and poisoned. In the summer of 1981 wolf tracks were finally seen again at Stoney Creek, 13 km. north of Banff townsite. Within a few years

they may be seen again in the Bow Valley. Unconfirmed sightings suggest they have already appeared in the Bow Valley in the vicinity of Johnston Canyon. In the meantime the only chance for a motorist to see a wolf is along the Icefield Parkway between Jasper townsite and the northern boundary of Banff Park.

Wolves closely resemble long-haired German Shepherd dogs, but are a touch larger. Average weight is 43 kg. They average about 154 cm. in length including their 40 cm. bushy tail. Shoulder height may be as tall as 1 m. The color of wolves varies; some may be snow white, others jet black, but most are a mixture between black and white. Females are 20% smaller than males. Unless you observe a wolf lifting its leg it is difficult to tell the difference between male and female.

Wolves are primarily carnivorous (meat

eaters). During the summer they will occasionally eat bits of grass, tender shoots, roots and berries, though rarely in any significant quanitity and always much less than the coyotes do.

The wolf is best known for killing and devouring big game animals, but often as not it must content itself with consuming small creatures such as mice, ground squirrels, gophers, rabbits and the occasional bird. They are most successful at bringing down large game when hunting in packs. On a long chase wolves can run about 32 kph and by working together in relays, generally manage to wear down their prey. Even in these situations it is usually only the young, old, or unhealthy animals that fall victim to the wolves. Animals in small herds can often fend off the wolves by striking out with their antlers or sharp hooves.

In their quest for food wolves may have a circuit well over 160 km. long which they might cover once or several times a month. The circuit often varies according to the migration patterns of other animals upon which the wolves depend for food.

Except during the period when they are rearing young, home is wherever they happen to lie down to sleep.

Wolves are capable of breeding at two years of age. When they choose a partner it is usually a life long relationship which may continue for 10 or 12 years. They generally breed early in March and have a gestation period of nine weeks. When the pups are ready to be born the bitch either digs out her own burrow in a steep bank, or, more likely remodels and enlarges an old badger or coyote burrow. One wolf even took over an abandoned beaver dam! There is nothing fancy about the inside, a simple dirt floor will do.

Litter size varies from four to ten pups but usually averages out to be six. The little fellows are fuzzy with blunt faces, short legs and skinny, pointed tails. Blind at birth, their eyes open about a week later. For the first three weeks they survive on mom's milk, then they gradually move to a meat diet which is initially partly digested by the parents. While confined to her den nursing the new litter the mother is kept supplied by her mate who hunts regularly. Not only does the husband provide, but other members of the pack often help out. The hunting grounds may be many miles away and wolves can hardly pack the groceries home in a shopping bag. They overcome the carrion carrying problem by cramming the meat into their stomachs and disgorging it when they get home.

By the time the pups are eight or ten weeks old they are gulping down fresh meat and developing teeth and jaws on tough bones. After two months they abandon the den and begin to range. At six months they already stand 60 cm. at the shoulder and have become fully experienced at running with the pack. Females often only breed every second year or third year so a family cohesiveness is maintained within the pack which usually comprises aunts and uncles as well.

Even though wolves raise large families and are the second most efficient mountain predator following the cougar, the fact that they do not breed every year helps to keep populations low. When they become abundant diseases such as rabies and distemper can quickly spread through the population with devastating results. Mange may cause their hair to fall out to such an extent that they cannot survive the winter cold, and food shortages affect wolves as they do primitive man.

Aside from encountering a grizzly bear, one of the greatest thrills which can befall a back-country camper is to hear the long low plaintiff howl of a wolf ringing through the cold dark mountain valleys at night as the campfire slowly dies out. One can almost guarantee that the reaction will be to sit up in the sleeping bag and quietly place more wood on the fire while listening closely for the next howl, always wondering if the wolves are drawing closer.

WOLVERINE

Wolverine H.U. Green

HE WOLVERINE IS CONSIDERED to be the meanest and most vicious of all the mountain mammals. They are nick-named "skunk-bears", resembling a bear which got shrunk in a hot wash and smelling like skunk which never went through the wash. The resemblance can be quite striking if one looks at the small stuffed black bear upstairs in the government museum in Banff. The bear was improperly mounted, snarling in a low crouch position. For all intents and purposes it looks more like a wolverine than a bear.

This largest member of the weasel family grows 1 m. long including its 22 cm. bushy tail. Males weigh 14-16 kg. and the slightly smaller females weigh only 10-13 kg. They stand about 38 cm. high at the shoulder. It is a testament to their ferociousness that these animals, less than one-tenth the size and weight of an average bear, have no known natural enemies. Not even grizzly bears care to take them on.

The long guard hairs on the wolverine's coat are unique; they do not ice up when condensation settles on them in winter. For this reason the fur is highly prized for hood and collar trimming on winter parkas.

Wolverines will eat almost anything and they do not even care if their meat is fresh or spoiled. Their main diet consists of rabbits, mice, ground squirrels, chipmunks, marmots and ground roosting birds such as grouse and ptarmigan. During the winter they rely heavily on rabbits though they will kill winter weakened sheep, deer and elk. No animal is too large for a wolverine to attempt to bring down, although it is not always successful. If desperately hungry they will go after porcupines.

Wolverines are shameless robbers. If they come upon a trapline they will eat the trapped animals and often steal the bait from unsprung traps, rarely getting caught themselves. They can climb, dig or gnaw their way into almost any building. Once inside a building they will sometimes tear apart everything they can get their paws on, as if out of sheer devilry. Bedding is ruined, pots and pans are scattered and defecation piles are left everywhere. When one comes upon a cabin visited by a wolverine one seriously entertains the alternative of burning it down instead of attempting to clean it up.

Anywhere in the mountains is potential wolverine range, from the lowest valleys to the highest alpine meadows. They travel incredible distances at a consistant loping gait which does not vary even on the steepest slopes. We once followed wolverine tracks on skis in a foot of fresh powder snow over two 2750 m. passes from Lake O'Hara to Moraine Lake. We encountered the fresh tracks early in the morning and followed them over one pass and down to the base of the next pass well before lunch. Looking up to the second pass we saw the tracks not only going over but coming back as well, then going off down another valley. As it turned out, the wolverine had bounded 18 km. and cleared two high passes through loose snow, stopped near Moraine Lake lodge to breakfast on a rabbit and come back 6.5 km. to clear the second pass again before disappearing down the other valley, all well before noon.

Wolverines appear to have some pattern to their ranging and possibly even pass on knowledge of good areas down through the generations. A biologist observed an adult and young visiting a fish camp at Baker Lake near Lake Louise in 1947. In the summer of 1975, while a park warden, I received reports of wolverines raiding fish camps in exactly the same spot they were reported twenty-eight years earlier.

Very few wolverines have been seen and, because they are so small and ferocious and can travel such incredible distances, little is known about their personal habits. Judging from sightings and tracks they always travel alone except for a brief courtship and mating period in February or March. Gestation period is guessed to be about two months. They do not construct fancy dens. An overhanging rock, the base of a hollow tree, or some dense coniferous foliage is a sufficient home for a female to stop at briefly to bear her young. A young pup was once found and estimated to be two days old. It was only 20 cm. long and weighed a mere 98 gm. yet it was already on its way to being a tough scrapper. By late fall the pups are two-thirds adult size and are off on their own to take on the world of winter.

The majority of reports concerning wolverines have a tendency to stress their bad points, and few people have tried to find the good in them. Mr. Green, a warden in Banff National Park, worked with wolverines for a Walt Disney production in the mid forties. He found that with time and patience it was possible to become friends with these ''ferocious'' animals. The wolverines which the film crew became familiar with did not emit any foul odours and did not display any aggression toward the people they came to know. One wolverine would even eat calmly from the hand of a crew member.

These men made numerous important observations contrary to the popular lore concerning wolverines. The handlers found the animals were clean in their personal habits. They ate only what would be expected for their size, and did not deserve the title of glutonous which their Latin name implies. Through some controlled testing the men concluded that eggs are also a part of the wolverine's natural diet. The animals were also extremely adept at climbing trees, but no one could conjecture why wolverines have this ability. Finally, and most important, the men established the fact that wolverines could be handled. To my knowledge, no one has attempted such an experiment again and it may be years before we come to really know the wolverine.

Metric Equivalent of weights and measures

Linear measure
1 inch = 2.54 centimetres
1 foot = 0.30480 metres
1 yard = 0.914399 metres
I mile = 1.6093 kilometres

Avoirdupois Measure
1 ounce = 28.349527 grams
1 pound = .453592 kilogram

Square Measure
1 sq. inch = 6.4516 sq. centimetres
1 sq. foot = 9.29034 sq. decimetres
1 sq. yard = .836131 sq. metre
1 acre = .40469 hectare
1 sq. mile = 2.59 sq. kilometres = 259 hectares

To convert kilometres to miles,
multiply by 0.62.

Rick Kunelius Ed Cavell

Rick Kunelius has worked as a Park Warden in Banff since 1973. He has also written *Ski Trails in the Canadian Rockies*.

Design: Scott Thornley, STDA
Art Production: Bruce Aitken, STDA
Typesetting: Crocker Bryant Inc.
Printing: Dai Nippon
Printed and Bound in Japan